FREEDOM
from
ANXIETY

A Deeper Approach to Healing

H A R R Y   K R O N E R

BALBOA.
PRESS

A DIVISION OF HAY HOUSE

Balboa Press books may be ordered through booksellers or by contacting:

Balboa Press
A Division of Hay House
1663 Liberty Drive
Bloomington, IN 47403
www.balboapress.com
1 (877) 407-4847

Because of the dynamic nature of the Internet, any web addresses or links contained in this book may have changed since publication and may no longer be valid. The views expressed in this work are solely those of the author and do not necessarily reflect the views of the publisher, and the publisher hereby disclaims any responsibility for them.

All client stories in this book had their names changed to protect their identity. Only the most relevant pieces of information related to the chapter have been included. All other identifying segments have been omitted to preserve the privacy and respect their own journey.

Any people depicted in stock imagery provided by Thinkstock are models, and such images are being used for illustrative purposes only. Certain stock imagery © Thinkstock.

Print information available on the last page.

ISBN: 978-1-5043-4318-3 (sc)
ISBN: 978-1-5043-4319-0 (e)

Balboa Press rev. date: 10/23/2015

Contents

Exercises

Dedication

This book is dedicated to YOU!

It is my intention, and hope, that you find inspiration, and openness to your own potential to be free of anxiety and achieve full self mastery in this lifetime. It is within your grasp.

Acknowledgement

This book could not have been written without the inspiration, wisdom, and experiences, of my dear clients. They have enriched me immensely, and I hope I have given them as much as they have given me. Each and every one of them provided me the opportunity to practice my passion, and be of service to the world in a way that is most gratifying to me. Thank you.

I deeply appreciate the support I received from my wife throughout the years, and in writing this book. Her ability to understand me could not be surpassed by any. I am grateful for her belief in me, even when sometimes I doubted myself.

I would also like to thank my editor, Roni Hornstein, and Balboa Press for assisting me in making this dream a reality.

Introduction

Anxiety is devastating the lives of millions across the U.S. and the world.

Imagine for a moment that you are feeling anxious. You have tried many things dealing with the feeling of anxiety. Developed all kinds of tactics to try and deal, or avoid, anxiety. Prescription medication and self-medication relieves the symptoms temporarily, but does nothing in the long term to the suppressed emotion and anxiousness. Most of them just mask it, numb you, or temporarily relieve it, only to return the minute it wears off. You avoid situations, people, and scenarios that might trigger it. Limiting your life further and further. It is always lurking in the background, or worse, it is taking over your life.

The solution lies in addressing the entire being and not just the symptoms. Reaching deep into healing, and re-creating self in a comprehensive yet gentle manner. Transcending spiritually, emotionally, mentally, and physically.

In my practice I have worked with hundreds of people suffering from a wide array of manifestations of anxiety. Some experienced deep traumatic events, others have been rattled by witnessing something, yet some others don't even know the source of their anxiety. There is so much to learn and unlearn in the process of freeing oneself from anxiety.

While working with my clients, I noticed that although they all are very unique and perceive things differently, there are some common threads to their experience. I developed the one on one program *Freedom from Anxiety* to address this need. In it, I teach people techniques, tools, and mindsets of how to free oneself of anxiety. However, I found myself repeating the concepts and perspectives that I find important in the process of transcending anxiety into personal power. I decided to write this book to encapsulate these ideas and healthier approach to oneself and the world.

My wish is to further explore the inner worlds, and what needs to shift in order to regain your personal power. The book explains the concepts and approach behind the actual exercises, tools, and revelations that are the core of the *Freedom from Anxiety* program.

I chose the inner perspective with the hope that it will speak to you as an experiencer of anxiety, and not just to your mind. We are so much more than just our heads. We are entire beings, and need to be approached in this way.

I wish you experience a paradigm shift as you read this material. Tap into your own inner strength that is disconnected by the enormity of the feeling of anxiety. Gain a wider perspective on the matter with a more comprehensive view and understanding on who you are, and recognize your own power to transcend into wellness and inner peace.

The goal is to help you create a deeper connection with your true being. The process of releasing yourself from this cycle is to reconstruct your personal beliefs, relationship with yourself, and trust in the world. A way that is free from the negatively charged emotions and events. Re-activating your source of strength, calm, and confidence.

What needs to change in order to accomplish that?

Everything needs to change. Not outside of you, but inside. The mechanism needs to be reset. You are still going to be you, just a cleaner, better version of yourself. Without all the triggers, suppressed emotions, and anxiousness that is bogging you down. A wholesome integration of self, allowing you to access more tools that already exist within you, that you simply forgot how to access.

In this book I explore the four natural phases to the process of freeing yourself from anxiety. Understanding the nature of anxiety. Shifting on all levels of your being. Reclaiming your power, and developing a new sense of self.

Phase one is the deeper understanding of the nature of anxiety. Gaining clarity of what is the cause, triggers, and how did it come to be. Recognizing the areas that need changing. Being honest and accepting of yourself and your situation.

Phase two is starting the shift from within and on all levels of your being; physically, emotionally, mentally, and spiritually or universally. Releasing the old, limiting beliefs. On the physical level - Learning how to REALLY relax -Breathing techniques, meditations, training yourself to go deeper. Releasing emotional charge from past events, and feeling safe. Releasing negative self talk from the mind, limiting beliefs and negative patterns of thinking. Opening yourself to higher wisdom, soul healing, and your place in the universe.

Phase three focuses on reclaiming your power. Learning those things that will help you regain mastery over life, powerful tools, habits and perspectives.

In phase four you are integrating fully to a new model of self. A new sense of self that is authentic and free of anxiety, fear, and doubt. Bringing deep appreciation to your support system, and growing into a fully integrated and independent version of yourself. Striding safely and confidently in the world.

These phases do not necessarily take a linear form, and in the process of freeing yourself you may jump back and forth between the phases. There is no right way or wrong way, just your way.

This is a process, and needs to be approached in this manner. It takes time. Allowing concepts and tools to mature and integrate into your new way of being - Free from Anxiety!

It is within our power to shift and change. We are not merely the passengers in our own life, although sometimes it feels this way. Shift that energy from your core, know that you have the power to make a change in your own existence. Life does not have to be so bleak or out of control. You have the capacity to change this way of being, just know it, it is within you. If you need assistance, we can do this together. I will help you and guide you through this process.

Anxiety will not loom so heavily over you - NO MORE. It is a process of self understanding, self clearing, cleansing and resetting our focus in life to the things we have forgotten; that we are powerful beings. We are the masters of our own lives. We have the capacity to shift any past event and cleanse the emotional baggage from its core, and not let it run our lives. It does not mean that unpleasant events did not take place. What it means is that we no longer let them run our lives. You have the power to change; make peace with yourself, and be free!

This is the dawn of a new day, embrace it!

PHASE ONE

Deeper Understanding
of Anxiety

The Challenge of Anxiety

You are a human being experiencing anxiety,
not anxiety experiencing a human being.

Anxiety is not an emotion, it is a comprehensive systemic response to deeper fear and distorted views of self and the world. Anxiety includes emotions, such as fear, hopelessness, panic, dread, trapped, loss of control, being judged, frustration, self loathing, anger, and more. It also includes the physiological responses to these emotions and beliefs in the form of elevated heart beat and blood pressure, increased speed of thought, release of stress hormones, and more.

However, these are the symptoms that stem from deeper subconscious structures of belief about yourself and the world. These distorted views and beliefs cause the trickling effect that we know as anxiety. There is nothing wrong with you, just your views and your reaction to them that got locked into your system at some point in time.

Most people experience anxiety to some level, however, some have the tendency to take it further, much further into a spiral that is devastating their lives in a truly damaging way. One of the most challenging aspects of anxiety is the fear of experiencing anxiety again. The length to which people will go to try and avoid it. The fear of feeling anxious is causing us to change our lives.

Let's have a deeper look at anxiety from the point of view of the experiencer.

Imagine you feel anxious, out of control, stressed out, feeling no way out of a situation, dreading the potential of something bad happening any moment. Your mind is racing, obsessing about a situation where you feel terrible, letting the mind race even faster in the hope that you will gain some control or be more ready when it happens. It might happen anywhere, anytime, or whenever you feel most vulnerable, and trapped.

You hate how it feels, the tightness in your chest, dizziness, the pit in the stomach the blood rushing through you and without warning. Anxious thoughts keep repeating and start to consume you, sometimes at a low level in the background, and sometimes taking over the brain entirely. You feel as if there is a hamster wheel in your head and it's spinning faster and faster, with no way of catching up.

You develop elaborate strategies in order to avoid any possible situation or memory that might trigger it. You keep busy trying to push away these anxious thoughts. However, they don't let go, they just wait until sleep time, and you just can't shut your brain off.

You walk around exhausted, irritated, and even more anxious. You start medicating yourself to sleep. Maybe with some pills, maybe with a few drinks before sleep, or maybe with other recreational drugs. Eating more throughout the day to avoid the fatigue, and just to get some instant relief. A sweet moment in a hectic day.

At this point it becomes a constant internal struggle. Desperate to get rid of it at any price. It seems like an endless, hopeless, catch up game in which you are doomed to never gain control.

People tell you to "let go", "stop worrying about it", and it just makes you even more frustrated. You think to yourself "If I could just let it go, you think I wouldn't?" Feeling alone, misunderstood and alienated from the world. "Nobody really gets me." You feel upset, frustrated and very anxious. There is no solution you can think of....

STOP!

Stop this vicious cycle!

Take a deep breath with me and let's get a clearer view on the matter. We get so easily caught in these spirals of doom that we lose ourselves and healthy perspectives on our lives.

There are no situations in our modern life that anxiety will help in dealing with better than a cool, calm mind and body. So let's slow down the crazy wheel and see how we can transcend anxiety into personal growth and self mastery.

Anxiety shows us that we are in discord with the world and ourselves. It alerts us to the fact that there is something that needs addressing and shifting within us. It helps you be more aware of things. Fear, and its hyper child, anxiety, cannot serve us right now. Realize that you are in need of an internal re-programming, and that's OK, it can be done. Anxiety is a red flag that needs addressing. It is a signal that, "I'm missing something here, if it makes me this anxious, I need to understand it better."

Anxiety is smaller than we think. We have the tendency to focus on something and when we focus on it, it seems bigger and occupies more space in our minds. It inflates in importance whether it is true or not. The more we focus on the anxiety and our challenges that stem from it, the bigger it feels, the more it looms over our lives and taints them with helplessness, hopelessness, and powerlessness.

Allow anxiety to fall back into a more appropriate place as an indicator, an early warning system, and not the actual problem. It is a signal that needs a wise and purposeful response. We might need the help of others in understanding and transcending it, and that's okay, too.

It is an opportunity for growth. Learning the pearls of wisdom that lay underneath the surface of every emotion you experience. Let's stop judging and over-analyzing ourselves for having anxiety, and let's start shifting it.

The shift doesn't happen in a day, there is a learning curve. Throughout the process of freeing ourselves from anxiety there will be some setbacks. It does not mean that you will never get rid of it, it simply means it is a process that ebbs and flows, until you fully cement yourself in the field of a newer you. It can take a week, three months, or a year. What matters is giving ourselves the space to shift and grow into a better version of ourselves, free of anxiety.

Understanding Emotions

"Know Thyself"

Our emotions are encapsulating enormous wisdom within them and it is essential to understand this wisdom so we may learn, grow, and expand.

After experiencing anxiety, we wish to rid ourselves of this feeling and anything related to it. However, every emotion has something to teach us. The key is that once the lesson has been learned and the wisdom absorbed into your heart and soul, it dissolves that feeling, that energy. The emotion does not need to be repeated, it is released from our system and the influence it has on us.

Emotions skew the direction of thoughts. Most people believe it is the thoughts that come first and the emotion follows, however, emotion then completely shifts you and your energies for a considerable amount of time. The emotion keeps you in a certain state, a certain vibe, and dictates all of your thoughts from that point on until another emotion appears, usually in a continued theme of the first one.

I'm sure you can think of many occasions in your life when something good happens, you feel this elation and things that before bothered you now seem unimportant because you feel so good. Thoughts tend to be optimistic, thinking brightly of the future. Your entire outlook on life seems hopeful, filled with possibilities and free of constraints. Your thoughts are free and filled with potential.

The reverse is also true, when suddenly you are feeling down, anxious, you are filled with negative thoughts and view life and your future in a bleak, hopeless and pointless outlook. It is not only what you feel, it is affecting all thought. If someone tells you when you are down to think of something good, it feels almost impossible, it is hard to even attempt to think positively about anything at that point.

An emotion will stay around and be triggered whenever something will remind you of when it was created. It is like a ball of energy that is created inside at a certain point in time. Until you figure it out, it will remain unprocessed and suppressed. The emotion and your subconscious are attempting to resolve and process. However, because you are vibrating on this level you WILL attract situations, people, and triggers that will urge you to process and understand it. This is the law of attraction that is working all the time.

The internal conflict accelerates. We wish to avoid it while other parts of us are trying to resolve it, but we are afraid of dealing with it. Avoidance and suppression perpetuate this struggle and lead us to change our behavior. We make the mistake in thinking that not feeling is better than feeling.

Common avoidance and numbing behaviors of this sort are, watching hours of TV, over working, spending too much time on the internet and social media, excess video or computer gaming, using drugs to calm yourself down either prescribed or recreational, drinking alcohol in excess, and in extreme cases starting to use hard drugs. Numbing ourselves for a few hours and calling it "relaxation." The emotions are numbed through yet another day, bottled up and unresolved.

Take a moment and notice what are your "go to" numbing behaviors?

There is more to understand about our emotions before we start facing them and healing them.

E-motion - Energy in Motion.

The challenge with anxiety and fear is that it feels so strongly stuck in us. We bottle up all these feelings and wedge them deep inside. We are held captive without motion because we are suppressing, and restricting the energy from flowing. Freedom from anxiety is the freedom from immobility, freedom from stagnation, stuckness, from lack of motion forward with ease and joy.

Let's have a look at some examples of freedom in emotions. Notice that feelings such as apathy has almost no motion, no movement, it is stale. Anger for example, has more motion than apathy or hopelessness, because anger is moving more energy. It is still negative, but there is action taken in Anger. From being completely hopeless, you decide to do something about it and engage in your personal power, even if at this point it in the reactive, negative range of emotions.

As we rise and start freeing the energy of emotions we experience better and better emotions. We reach the feeling of wanting and longing. We want our situation to get better. However, wanting and seeking something focuses on the fact we do not have what we want, and creates frustration. We all want inner peace, but don't get stuck in the WANTING because it is much lower on the scale of freedom.

Moving into the positive range of emotions, brings the sense of lightness and freedom. Feelings such as enthusiasm, confidence, cheerfulness, etc.; feelings that you can sense move you without restriction. The heaviness of negativity is lifted. We actually feel the lightness inside.

Ultimately we have the feelings of acceptance and peace, and bliss. These emotions feel almost buoyant. We feel so light and free that it feels like floating. There is free movement without restriction. Peace has all the freedom, all the power, and potential energy without restriction.

Moving higher through the energetic range of emotions is a movement towards freedom.

An entire new field in psychology called "Positive Psychology" has been created in the past decade and a half is showing how systematically you can move yourself to a more positive range of emotions. It is natural and it is important to know that you are capable of moving yourself up that scale and exist in a higher state of energy and freedom. We constantly fluctuate in this range, but you can permanently move yourself to a higher base point when you start the process of releasing and understanding of emotions.

The Spirit of Emotions

Let's take an even higher view point on experiencing emotions. It is important to remember that you are here to experience, learn, and grow; that is the sum of why we are here on earth. It is one of the big questions in life.

"Why am I here?"

The universal answer is: "To experience, learn, and grow."

What you experience and what your particular mission and lessons are vary from person to person, but the purpose is as universal as can be.

We cannot experience life fully without the emotions. They are like enhancers of an experience. Life on earth has one of the highest level of emotional intensity in our universe. Therefore, experiencing emotions can get overwhelming at times, however, it is what we came here to do.

So allow yourself to know that it's OK to feel fear, anxiety, apprehensiveness, desperation. Those strong negative feelings provide enormous contrast to positive feelings that we naturally yearn for, such as, inner peace, joy, enthusiasm, and bliss. These positive emotions become even more powerful because we know how it feels to be on the other end of the emotional scale.

Feelings and emotions are not permanent, they can continually flow. It does not mean that you will need to be constantly going back to negative emotions in order to enjoy the positive ones. You have already done your share in the negative side, now it is time to transcend and learn the wisdom stored in these emotions. Learn how to overcome the challenges and live on a higher vibration where things flow with greater ease. Do not curse fear and anxiety, but use them as reference points in your experience in life. Know that from this point on you do not have to feel them again, you already had this experience, and now you are ready to transcend.

We will revisit the spiritual purpose of negative emotions in the chapter, "Shifting the Soul."

Understanding Fear

*Fear is designed to be the protector
of life, not the limiter of life*

Fear is our worst enemy, it stops us from being us. Fear is one of the most devastating forces in our human existence. We stop ourselves for a multitude of fears, and social programming that are limiting us in so many ways. We respond to fear in several ways, either fight, flight or freeze.

Fighting what we fear is causing havoc in our world today and throughout the ages. Let's look at some examples. Fear of people who are not like you, leads to hatred, racism, and ethnic cleansing. It is the fear, or feeling of threat of those that are different taking over your lifestyle, religion, comfort that brings out this ugly response to fear. Hitler's campaign against the Jews, Gypsies, and Communists, was purely based on fear of these people endangering the German way of being as he saw it. This fear still brings devastation in the world that is filled with intolerance and violence that is based on fear.

The more aggressive reaction to fear is more common among men, who respond to certain frustrations and anxiety with anger, directed towards themselves or those around them.

Moving away from the aggressive, fighting reactions to fear, we are focusing in this book on the debilitating reactions to fear by freezing or wishing to flee the situations, circumstances caused by feeling fear and anxiety.

What I found through the many accounts of my clients that the fear of having an anxiety attack at the wrong place and the wrong time, or having it at all, is the worst fear of all. This fear of feeling an anxiety attack to this level again is an enormous internal motivation to do anything in your power and avoid so many things, activities, people, situations, and locations in life. This is a tremendous limiter of life. We fear the emotions that we predict we will feel, and will do anything to avoid those feelings.

So how is fear created?

As suggested in the question, fear is a creation. Most of it is created unintentionally and unconsciously because a part of us is sensing a certain threat to our existence, whether real or just perceived. This perception of fear is shaping our experience at that moment. It is tying the situations with the sense of fear, creating a strong bind between the two. Our beautiful minds learn to avoid the perceived danger in the future.

The problem arises when we do this based on perceived fear when truly there is no real threat. We tend to over-use this life protecting mechanism and apply it too liberally. We have reached a point in which it just went a little too far. Leading us to feeling anxious more often than not.

Fear has been allowed free reign over us, and it becomes a source of limitation in our lives. It was not meant to be a source of limitation, simply protection. For example, it is obvious we need to be careful along the edge of a cliff, but do experience the beautiful views from the cliff. Obviously, with basic safety in mind. Its role and purpose is to serve as the protector of life so you can experience life to the fullest without losing it before your time. Some people have a stronger tendency to do so, and it means it needs to be managed more carefully.

The purpose of us having this life, is to experience. It is your role to be the experiencer. When we start to limit ourselves too much, our soul suffers and feels constricted. We intuitively know this is wrong. Experiencing and allowing our souls to experience being human is what we are here to do; to live, love, and matter.

I like to give the example of having a pet. Some say, "Why even bother if you will experience the pain of them dying before you." If you have ever lost a pet, you know there is real grief that you feel. But we simply choose love over loss. The years of love, joy and experiences, both bad and good that a pet brings into our lives is worth the pain and suffering we might experience at the end of their lives. We are deeply enriched, and through this experience of growth and expansion we expand our souls.

At this point in time, it is important to allow fear to return to its place, as the protector of life, and not the limiter of life. We have allowed it to grow to more than its design. We can free ourselves of fear and the anxiety that we experience as a result of an event that got locked-in with the emotion of fear. It is a process of untangling. Allowing ourselves to love life again in spite of social expectations, bad programming, and our own emotional-memory locking system, that outgrew its design.

We are not in imminent danger when we are about to give a presentation, when we drive our car, ride a plane, see someone vomit or leave our house. Can we die in any of these events? Absolutely, but you can also die while watching the TV, while sleeping (lovely way to go), while walking to the bathroom, or eating your food. If it is your time to go, you will go, not before, not after. We all have a designated point of departure and if you start thinking of it, probably someone died in every situation in life, any circumstance. But it does not mean we will never do this activity, it is impossible to live life this way.

Don't misunderstand me, I look both ways before I cross the street because it makes sense, I drive with caution, making sure I read other drivers that are sharing the road with me, it makes sense, but I do it without fear, anxiousness, or anger, just caution, and the basic need for preservation of life. This is your goal, to function and go through life without the constant anxiety looming over you; to be truly free and live life without an overwhelming sensation of fear.

So how is it achieved? I take my clients on a journey and help them connect with their inner wisdom. While connecting with the pure stream of consciousness from higher within themselves, I simply ask, will you die in this form that you fear? (whatever it is for the client: airplane crash, automobile, riding over a bridge, etc.) and the answer most of the time is "NO!" It is an illusion we have created, or an event / information that got locked in us through fear. Do not worry, I would not actually let you know how you die or when, it takes the fun out of life. This type of information is usually hidden from us. However, the higher self can tell you how you will not die. This information does not break any universal laws.

We can take it further and apply to other manifestations of anxiety such as social situations, the people who suffer from this form of anxiety, fear the loss of control over their body, in the form of a panic attack. Re-experiencing an event that got locked with fear, in this case, the fear of it repeating, the fear of experiencing a panic attack with all its unpleasant physical sensations, and public embarrassment of you having them. It feels like you are going to die any second and that is obviously not desired by anyone. However, it is still fear that is misplaced and limits us from life and normal functioning.

The Need to Control
& Powerlessness

Anxiety comes from deep distrust in the natural flow of life.

Are you a "control freak?" Were you ever called that?

Why do we feel the need to control?

We get the most anxious, upset, frustrated, and angry when we try to control things that are out of our control - such as other people or situations. We feel obligated to control the situation or person because we fear it will get out of control and not result in the desired expectation.

It is easy to feel that need to control when we are responsible for the outcome in some way, at work, with our children or partners. My children could attest to the fact that I was pretty terrible at this, especially in the beginning before I figured out what is the biggest trigger of this need to control. Beyond the obvious of not wanting to let my children get out of control, it is important to notice what is usually at its base - you guessed it - FEAR!

Obviously we need to guard our children, but my fear of them not succeeding, or showing traits that I know will not help them in life are difficult for me as a healer to let them be. It is the fear of their failure or future failures that drove me to fear some of their actions and behaviors and my great push to remedy it out of them. The worse ones are those traits I know came from me, and I know that they caused me much suffering and difficulty and I was trying desperately for them to not have to go through the same difficulties.

I know many parents do this either consciously or unconsciously, but it brings us a great urge to control our children instead of just influencing them and allowing their journey to unravel with our support and not control.

It is important to separate what is truly under our control and those things that are not. There is a simple rule in this.

You can control yourself, but you cannot control others!

You can influence others, but you really cannot control them in any way, they have their own free will, as many parents of young adults and teenagers will tell you with great frustration. You will need to see them fail, suffer, make mistakes, and all you can do is guide and advise them. Another good catch phrase I learned in the business world is to stick to what you can truly control, in other words

"Control the controllable."

So let's focus on what you can control - you!

The challenge with anxiety is that most people who suffer from it do not feel they are in control of themselves when they feel anxious. The basic feeling of control over oneself suddenly takes a turn for the worst and the trust in our own capacity to respond correctly is deeply shaken. I will address this more fully in phase three about regaining your power, but for now let's elaborate on the need to control

The best metaphor I give my clients is driving on the road. It is the ultimate example that all you can truly control is your own vehicle and yourself. You cannot control other people's reactions, attention or vehicle. You can influence them by alerting them or reading their moves, but not dictating their choices as your own. You can respond to them, but you cannot control them. We actually are all in our own bubble (of metal and glass) and those small universes interact with each other surprisingly well.

So our best course of action on the road is to drive respectfully, pay attention to the road and others, be at peace about it, and make it to our destination. Sounds simple right? I know it's not so for all of us, especially if your particular anxiety revolves around traveling.

Let's break it down and make it more tangible. Open your mind and without judgment answer these questions?

EXERCISE: Understanding the Anxiety and Need to Control.

What are you afraid of? Take a moment and see what is it you fear?

Do you fear you will not be listened to? Acknowledged? Not be valued as a person, or worker? Fear that what you are responsible for will not be accomplished? Fear that you will have a panic attack in similar situations? Fear you will die, or be injured? Etc., etc.

There are many fears. So what is that fear that you experience when you think of...?

The first step of moving away from anxiety is understanding it fully and in depth.

Now let's take this exercise a few steps deeper:

- Sit down quietly and take a long deep breath and exhale even slower. Allow the feeling of release as you exhale again. Allow your eyes to close between the questions and even now. Feel how you can simply dump all the clutter from your head into a mental waste basket next to you as you exhale further and further. Take your time and slow down, shift into neutral. Allow yourself to fade gently and ask these questions free of judgment:
- What is the general area in life I feel anxious about? (work, kids, partner, health, wellness, financial...)
- Why do I have the urge to control it?
- What is the fear behind the need to control it? (sit with it for a little while, allow yourself to process)
- Where does this fear come from? (certain emotion, memory...)
- When did I feel this feeling or fear before?
- What does it teach me?
- What else can I learn about this?
- What can I do next time I start feeling this way?
- Can I let go of it now, can I make peace with it?
- Is there any action I need to take?

Take a moment and write the insights that came through. Do not be harsh with yourself or others. Repeat this exercise with every known trigger, or anxiety. You will be amazed at how much you can clear with this exercise. We will take it further in the next few phases.

Understanding Attachments

Attachment to ideas of perfection is the source of much of our anxieties.

We are attached to many false perceptions of perfection. Archetypal models of who we *should* be, created by ourselves or others. We are attached to this "Perfect" self that was engrained into us by society and family, but mostly by ourselves internalizing all these expectations and turning them into a solid ideal-self that has been antagonizing us ever since it was created.

Many social anxieties stem from this attachment and wish to adhere to its promises of receiving love, promotion, and acceptance by "good behavior" for following other's expectations of us. How we want to be perceived based on what we try to project to the world and our fear that we do not do perfectly. We allow ourselves to feel that the love, affection, and desire of others to be with us will depend only on our ability to be that perfect self.

This mistake of conditioning others' love and acceptance only if we become that archetypal self brings much anxiety and fear of not being accepted, loved, or wanted by others. The need for acceptance is heightened in people, and leads us to do all kinds of things and trying to match that perfect ideal and on the way lose our authentic self and bits of joy in life. Therefore, it feels like anxiety robs us of our joy and happiness. However, it is not anxiety, but the fear of not adhering to our false sense of ideal self, and our attachment and disappointment in ourselves for not being perfect.

I would like to expand on this because it is important to internalize and change our story, to reflect our authentic self, not false ideals of self.

There is a positive intention behind expectations from us as children. Many children feel tremendous pressure from their parents to stand up to their demands. This is a negative reflection of a positive intent that parents have from their children. The positive intent is seeing the potential within the child and trying to show the growing child that they can do more with their lives and achieve; to see and step up to their true potential. However, this often gets done in a negative way of pressure and demand on the child in the hopes that it will propel them to do better. This negativity gets internalized and creates an idealized self, and the never ending self-loathing, resentment and lower self-esteem that stems of not being that idealized self.

This leads to making mistakes as adults. People often mistake goals and aspirations with false self-images. I know I have done it many times throughout my life. If you say to yourself, "I will be happy when..." you are already depriving yourself of joy and authenticity from this moment, until it is accomplished (if ever). This is prevalent with highly successful people. Once they reach a goal they have laid out for themselves, whether it is financial or a certain position, they expect the feeling of satisfaction and fulfillment they envisioned. Only to discover a certain emptiness once it is reached. They feel like a fraud. Very quickly they will set another goal with the hopes of really feeling satisfied, and complete, once they reach the next level. It is good to be inspired and take action, however not in this way.

This is an erroneous view of perfection and ideal self. It is just an elaboration of the same sense you have, thinking that life is like a painting that must be completed, and until it is completed you will be unsatisfied, thereby, linking your happiness with a certain conditioning. At that moment you have sentenced yourself to unhappiness until it is accomplished, with a certain sense of anxiety propelling you towards it.

The other side of the coin is letting go of this false conditioning of happiness, acceptance and love. Recognizing that you are an ever-evolving painting that will never be finished but simply continues to flow and become ever richer with the experience of life. Every experience is another brush stroke to the masterpiece of life.

Attachment to false ideal-selves is the wrong propelling system to success. However, we also know that we should not stop growing and shifting. We must do it out of joy, inspiration, and amazement in the world; create goals as adventure to embark on, without being attached to a particular end result. This will lead us to mistakenly depriving ourselves of love and acceptance.

So take a moment and look upon yourself and notice what ideal selves are you attached to?

How is it limiting your joy and happiness right now?

I laughed when I first did this exercise, at my own unconscious attachment to a false ideal of perfection. How much anxiety it was creating inside. So many expectations and judgments that are fully self-imposed.

It is time to shift out of attachment and connect with your authentic self. Connect to what brings you deep joy and satisfaction in the moment, not in some distant point in the future. Engage in goals settings and strive not for perfection but for the best expression of self. I work with many clients that are anxious about their direction in life. We work on finding their passions, joys, and interests, no matter how far-fetched. It does not matter at that point how they will get there, but first dream without limits. The "how" will be resolved later. First have a vision that is close to your heart, and don't be attached to a particular end result because it might change and evolve to different manifestations than you expected.

See the world on a grander scale. It is self-growth and movement in the direction of ultimate self-manifestation, not a limiting designation of profession, or other socially accepted jobs. True goals represent your inner desires. General directions to strive for, but not locked into specifics. Striving towards a clearer and purer version of yourself, not external landmarks.

However, the opposite happens quite often. Many of us idealize others and simply cannot see ourselves as even getting close to the possibility of us becoming that ideal self. I remember when I first read Deepak Chopra's *The Seven Spiritual Laws of Success* I was amazed at the concepts and the new way of thinking. I thought to myself how could I ever just think this way all the time? It seemed so far away from my consciousness at the time and although I was deeply inspired, I had that nagging feeling that I would never be able to think or be this way. Seven years later I read the book again (I highly recommend you read it, again), and found that I understood the thinking much easier, but had not implemented it into my life on the practical level. It still felt out of reach, however, inside the idealization of being so spiritual and inept in writing started to shift. I hoped that at some point I would be able to do that and teach it to others. The attachment to that ideal was loosening, but I still thought, "I will never be able to make a living out of it" so the thought of the ideal still limited me and my dream making me feel inadequate in so many ways.

Since then I have gone through many more moments of misinterpretation and attachments to false ideal selves, and feeling very inadequate based on that ideal self that I have created of others, constantly comparing myself to others in my field that are doing better, bringing much anxiety of how the hell am I going to make it to their level from my lowly point. I starting dreaming of such success and level of mastery, but doing so out of a feeling of desperation and anxiety and not in pure inspiration. I knew I had the potential and the internal power to do so, but did it in completely the wrong way, bringing much anxiety, anger, and envy.

Years have gone by and I have developed in my field and worked on releasing myself from these attachments. Letting go of these false idealizations of self and others. Breaking away from that cycle of anxiety that consumed me early in my career. Now, I only see people as how close they are to their own journey; making sure I am free of attachment to expectations of myself, my children, and others. Knowing that people are on their own path, some of them are further along the path and some are not, and some are yet to discover their path and that's okay. Now I follow my authentic self and allow myself to unravel in MY way, without comparison, or falsehood. It is freeing beyond measure. I have recently read the book again, and saw it as the beautiful masterpiece it is. I now not only think that way, I am that way, for the most part. There is always room for improvement.

I remember one of the key sayings that broke this attachment to idealization of others for me is that in order to teach second grade math you do not have to hold a Master's degree in education or math, you simply can be a third grader. I say this with deep respect and appreciation to teachers. The better trained your teacher, the better your possibilities of learning, and more in depth. However, you can learn or teach others that are just one step below you in a certain subject. In the same way that in the business world you train a new employee by a skilled and experienced employee. It does not have to be the CEO or head of the department. So let go of the idealization that you have to have an enormous amount of education or training in order to start helping people in any area. That is a false attachment, you just need to do your personal best.

So allow yourself to think with kindness, "What am I attached to?"

"How much anxiety am I imposing on myself and my surroundings because of these attachments?"

"How much gentler can I be on myself or others if I let go of it?"

Deep Root Cause / Core event

Every anxiety has its core, Whether you are experiencing a troubling event currently that is causing you great anxiety or whether it is a constant barrage of anxieties, each anxiety has an emotional core that needs healing. Even when you are experiencing an obvious crisis such as a sick loved one, trouble in your relationships, loss of a job, etc. These always have an emotional charge that is created then and there or somewhere in your past.

The core event can be experienced, witnessed or vicariously absorbed as perceived fear or anxiety. I remember when I was studying trauma at the university, the stories I read of terrible things that happened to people, truly affected me. I believe it was during that time, that I consciously decided that I would help people let go of trauma in some way because otherwise they would be only be a shadow of themselves. I remember reading about rape and incest and felt absolutely horrid about it, not because it was my personal experience, but because I saw how devastating it can be to the entire being on all levels. It can destroy people.

I have helped many people with severe traumatic experiences, and many of these experiences cause PTSD, anxiety, and many other manifestations. As hard as these experiences might be, it does not mean that every anxiety is born out of big traumas alone. Even mini trauma such as suddenly getting startled or frozen can be a shock to your system of beliefs, your view of yourself, other people, and the world. There is a broken, shattered discrepancy between the way you viewed your life, the world, and the event that just took place, and how you perceive it.

It changes you, and it changes you to the core, and until you assimilate it and heal it, you are broken, and feel a great sense of disharmony and fear. Every anxiety is born out of trauma, whether real or perceived it does not matter, because it becomes real to you.

At that moment you have charged a memory, an event, with the enormous power of emotion. At that moment you have changed inside, down to your DNA and the wiring in your brain. Only in recent years has the research of DNA shown that our DNA is not as static as once thought. It changes with what we eat, do for a living, think, and suffer. Certain genes get activated and de-activated. It is energetically ingrained into your structure. It is imperative that you heal you anxiety before you move it down through your DNA to your children.

Much anxiety is passed from one generation to another. It is done through your DNA and at the moment of conception you transfer not only your DNA, but your energetic imprint that includes your experiences, as well. Which genes are expressed in your parents' DNA can be transferred to you? The sources of your anxiety might come from further back than your own life. It can come from before birth when your mother was carrying you and when she felt joy, you felt those happy hormones flowing through you blood, and when she felt fear, and anxiety, the same occurs. But let's not resort to blaming our parents once again. We can do something about it.

It is important to know that we truly cannot change the core event. What we can change is our perception and perspective of it. Changing the emotions you feel while experiencing similar thoughts and memories. It is our goal to completely neutralize the negative effect you feel about the core event. Many people who come to me shudder at the thought of even thinking about the event or anything that reminds them of it. However, after some good internal work they can bring the memory into their thinking without feeling any fear, anxiety, and other negative feelings such as anger or helplessness they might have felt previously.

There are many ways of accomplishing this neutralization, and it requires great finesse with someone's feelings and thoughts. I will not list it here because I believe that this work cannot be completed without learning them thoroughly. Best results require the assistance of someone outside of you, to provide you with the shift in perspective and support you need at this crucial moment of healing.

Core events happen to be more interesting than you might think and may teach you more about yourself than you could imagine. The key lies in the healing and completing of the learning that needs to take place. Every emotion and anxiety has something to teach you; there is wisdom in every emotion. There are greater perspectives and levels of learning that are exceptionally hard to tap into by yourself. But even if it eludes you right now, it does not mean that it is pointless or just a menace. No matter what happened and when, there is growth waiting to take place within you. There is beauty in every emotion, embrace yourself, you are more beautiful, and interesting than you think. An internal shift is in your cards.

PHASE TWO

Shifting from Within

Shifting the Body

We all know how unpleasant anxiety feels. It manifests differently depending on the source of anxiety and on each individual's tendencies. Some anxiety is constant and low level, and some is explosive and overwhelming. Whether you suffer from one or both, it is ruining our body. It manifests in many different ailments from skin rashes, small discomforts, and on to full fledge major diseases. It is imperative that we address it and shift our body away from the effects of anxiety.

There are many methods of calming your body, mind, and soul and it is essential to know that you can influence the entire being from each and all of these channels. Our physical body grows accustomed to living with a certain level of stress and anxiety. We get used to maintaining a physical body that is harboring stress and anxiousness without even noticing it.

One of the great indicators of how your body is doing is through the breath. Take a moment now and notice how deep is your breath? If you have a rapid, shallow upper chest breath you are gearing your body towards a stressful state of being. Yes, it feeds itself in both ways. Anxiousness causes you to breathe this way, and breathing this way brings your body to feeling under stress. Break that habit, and bring awareness just to taking slower deeper breaths from your belly. Doing so sends a signal to the body and then now it can relax and calm down. Engaging the Para-sympathetic hormonal response that brings calm and normal functioning to the body. The more you do it, the calmer you get. It is a subtle but effective way of shifting the body to a better state very easily.

EXERCISE - 7/11 Breathing Pace:

Seven - eleven breathing exercise is VERY helpful anywhere and anytime. The more you do it the better you will feel throughout the day.

Let's do it together. Take a VERY SLOW breath in counting until seven. VERY SLOWLY exhale to the count of eleven.

You will find that at first it is hard to do, however after several breaths it becomes easier and easier. Start practicing this rate of breath and it will immediately slow down the body to a more pleasant state. It shifts your entire body from an elevated state of alarm to a deeper and calmer state of being. You are commanding the body to be at peace. The longer you are at this state the easier it is to stay calm; the more breathing room you will have to deal with things without the added "bonus" anxiety. In fact, it creates a larger buffer zone between you and anxiety. It literally creates breathing room.

Another very important thing to notice is WHERE you hold the anxiety in your body. I am not referring to the point of a full panic attack, but to your regular daily anxiousness. Many people hold it in the belly, or solar plexus, around the heart, back, or neck. Some individuals have two major areas of tightness. You can usually sense an area that is tighter than others, it is more constricted or simply feels as if there is a knot there. It is very important to notice this because it has two major implications to your health and awareness.

The area that harbors the anxiousness tends to constrict proper blood and energy flow to those areas. If the anxiety is left untreated for months or years it can cause major health problems to organs in that region. For example, many people that hold the anxiety in the belly start developing major digestive issues if left untreated, which may cause a new source of anxiety and worry.

People who tend to hold it in the heart area may start developing heart problems or esophagus issues. I used to hold my anxiousness in the solar plexus, and have had asthma for many years. Once I started taking care of my anxiety in a deeper way, the asthma was reduced significantly. Now, I need no medication on a regular basis. However, I still notice if I am starting to feel a gentle tightness in that region because this awareness is key to taking care of the anxiousness before it develops further. When this happens an internal flag pops up and tells me there is something that needs addressing and I must understand it more fully. Give it the attention it deserves.

That is why awareness of where we hold anxiety has important implications to our physical health. It also can serve as an indication of how well you let go of things. After establishing a clear point of reference, you will be able to notice the anxiety before you even recognize it mentally, and that is a wonderful gift of the body, signaling to us that there is something to address. So thank your body for being a wonderful warning system. Do not treat the tightness as a curse, but as a gift. Listen to the body more carefully and it will reward you with more internal ease, and not dis-ease.

One of the first things that I teach my clients is exercises in relaxation. Many of them have not been able to be fully relaxed in years, other than a few fleeting moments of calmness. As I do a long and pleasant relaxation with them they are opening themselves to re-learning how it really feels to be deeply relaxed. These deep relaxations are best one on one, where I can gauge how deep you are, and take you into a pleasing trance of wellness, peace, and calm. This creates that base reference point of being truly relaxed.

Many clients come to me and say, "I can never relax," and some do take longer than one session to build the trust and allow themselves to fully relax. It is vital to learn how to relax deeply. I, myself, used to be very hyper, and impatient, with a tendency for nervousness. It took me a very long time to learn how to relax and let go, and I thank hypnosis deeply for creating this opportunity within me, so I could become all that I am today and realize that hypnosis is the most wonderful key to our subconscious and our soul.

Do not be discouraged by your attempts with relaxation CDs. Your state of being is slightly different every time you listen. It is hard to follow a pre-recorded experience that does not address how you feel at this particular moment. There is something about the presence and energy of someone guiding your experience in the moment that liberates you to truly experience it fully within yourself. I highly recommend you do it even over the phone. I still recommend pre-recorded meditations and relaxations, but it needs to be an additional practice and exercise, not your sole practice.

Once this level of relaxation is established, it does not mean that you will not experience anxiety anymore, but it allows the body to learn how it feels to be very relaxed, and then you can repeat it more often, now. It is like learning how to ride a bike, no matter how many people will describe and explain to you how to do it, you need to experience it yourself. That way your muscle memory is activated and you fully comprehend the sensation viscerally.

There is an important element to doing more relaxations from this point on. Your entire level of anxiousness is reduced significantly, and even without addressing the core issues, yet, you already start to enjoy the effect of being more relaxed in your daily life. Things that used to irritate, annoy or bother you, do not phase you as much or take much longer to reach that point. You build a certain "immunization" to daily stressors and that is precious.

The most important thing you can do is make it your daily routine. Same as exercising your body needs to be done on a continuous basis and not only once a week. It is like a muscle, and it will only get stronger and become easier and easier.

A more tangible way of measuring the success of daily relaxations is through creating a scale from zero to ten of your current level of anxiety. "Zero" meaning no anxiety and "Ten" meaning a full blown panic attack. So let's say that you got used to living with a five or a six on a daily basis. Daily meditation will bring it down to a one or two, providing you with a lot more leeway, and room before reaching a five or six level, again, or even higher in case of a triggering event. It will simply rise slower or reach a lower point on the scale. Creating this buffer zone allows you to manage anxiety a lot easier. Gives you the opportunity to be in charge, having power over it, without that awful sensation of losing control.

The next step is learning quicker tricks and new positive tools that assist you in a moment of need. We anchor it into your conscious and subconscious mind. It reminds you how calm you can be with a click of your fingers and a deep breath, or any other physical cue you give yourself in order to activate this calmness on demand. In Neuro-Linguistic Programming it is called "an anchor". This method brings comfort to many as it reminds them that they are in charge of their anxiety and not the other way around.

There are many more cool little tricks you can create to help you feel more relaxed energetically. It is remarkable how effective it is. However, I believe it needs to be taught properly, so you can viscerally know how it feels in the body and around you.

EXERCISE - Melting Ice Block:

I want to thank Joe Schectman for teaching me this one on our way back from a conference while sitting at an airport. It is simple, effective, and you can do it anywhere and anytime.

1. Imagine you are holding a block of ice between your hands (hold them out as if you are really doing it). Don't be shy no one is looking.
2. Now transfer the issue/challenge, lump of anxiousness you feel and whatever emotions, stories, and feelings you have about it - into the block of ice. Really feel like it is flowing from your heart, body, and mind into that block of ice, as if there is an invisible flow that drains through your arms and hands, outside of you, and into that block of ice. Do it now until it is completed!

3. Once it is transferred into the block of ice, start melting it with your mind and allow the hands to slowly come closer together as the problem or issue is melting away.
4. Allow it to continue at its own pace until your hands touch each other, speeding up the melting process allowing all those issues to melt away.
5. Let it melt away until the palms of your hands fully melted the block away.
6. Take a deep breath and notice how you feel about the issue/challenge/anxiousness, now.

Many think that these tools are purely visualization exercises, however, I include it in the physical level chapter because I believe people need to FEEL it in their body, flowing through them, to make it more powerful and able to recall how it feels more than anything else. You activate it energetically. Learning how to do these energy exercises will bring you further along the way into wellness.

Physical Care

The body is one of our main concerns when we have anxiety. We simply do not want to feel an anxiety attack ever again. We do not want to feel the loss of control over our body and feeling all those symptoms of anxiety; quickening of the breath, the pit in the stomach, flush of sweat and dizziness, etc.

This complete sense of loss of control is one of the hardest aspects of anxiety. The problem is that most people get desperate and at this point simply do not want to feel at all. In fact, most people that come to me simply say, "I don't want to feel this way, anymore. I don't want to have those feelings."

The worst case scenario comes when some self-medicate in the wish to avoid feeling anxiety and resort to abusing prescription drugs, alcohol, cigarettes, recreational drugs, and some go all the way and use hard drugs such as heroin. All in the wish to not feel, numb the anxiety or get a temporary relief from anxiety. Sound extreme? Unfortunately, this is a reality for millions of people.

So let's not punish our body and heart for feeling anxiety, and start caring for the body. It will make you feel better, anyway, regardless of the anxiety. Do not give up on caring for yourself because you feel overwhelmed, it will bring you a step closer to overall wellness.

Developing good routines surrounding, sleep, exercise, healthy eating, spending time in nature are very important for your daily well-being. Every person is unique and it is valuable to create a routine that is best for you. Experiment with it, tweak existing routines and see how they support your health and wellness.

Anxiety symptoms are most evident in the body with the production of cortisol. That is the hormone of stress, fight or flight. The more anxious you are, the more cortisol is poured into your body. This affects your entire body in a negative way, causing adrenal fatigue.

There are many ways to help the body not produce so much cortisol or burn it out of the body and shift to positive feelings such as bliss and joy, through another hormone - endorphin, that is released in the body while exercising.

Exercise varies from person to person. Engage in physical activity that feels good and that you enjoy. A moderate to brisk walk in nature is very beneficial on many levels. There are many body-mind types of exercise such as yoga, tai chi, Qigong, that really bring great relief without being too intense on the body. Traditional exercise is also recommended, a good twenty minutes workout at the gym or cardio exercises can do wonders for your health in general and directly reduces stress and anxiousness. It is considered the natural fountain of youth, and for a good reason, too.

Eating well is another important factor in shifting physical symptoms of anxiety. Avoid sugar and carbohydrates in large quantities. They create sugar highs and lows, Sugar lows create an unpleasant sensation in the body that feel similar to the symptoms of anxiety. Avoid caffeine, as it excites your body too much and brings more anxious thoughts, along with the raised blood pressure that is causing you to feel more anxious.

These are basic concepts, and most people are aware of them, but focus on the challenge of squeezing yet another activity into their already busy day, forgetting how good it feels after a nice walk in nature, and how it literally burns the anxiety away. Adding these activities and eating consciously actually gives you more power and vitality to deal with the rest of your life, not the other way around. Having power over certain areas in life makes it easier to transfer this confidence to more and more areas. If you can easily turn this part of your life to a winner, the easier it will become to move forward in other areas.

Maintaining a healthy body is essential and, although we know it does not solve all of your anxiety issues, it is important to support your being on all levels. Anxiety will not be completely resolved if you choose to neglect one of these four levels of who you are, body, heart, mind, and soul. The better the body feels, the stronger the life force. The stronger the life force, the more power you have to overcome any challenges in your way. It is another way of expressing love to yourself, taking care of you, and that is very important in your healing process.

Sleep

Sometimes it is hard to notice your own anxiousness. It is an undercurrent of worry and anxiety that flies under the radar. However, sleep is one of those indicators that makes it easy to recognize you are anxious or stressed. Even if it is very deep under the surface, your subconscious will bring it up during this time at night, and restless sleep will rule the night if you do not address and heal those issues.

Sleep is a major challenge to many. I remember that during a sleep workshop I conducted the biggest complaint people had was their inability to shut their brain down. The second most common complaint was waking up in the middle of the night and milling problems, issues, work, and all the other anxious inducing thoughts.

The sad part of it is that people seek chemical relief from the symptom of lack of sleep. They are led by the desperate need to rest and sleep, and who could blame them. Without sleep we cannot function. So an immediate relief is medication. The amount of sleep drugs distributed in the U.S. alone is alarming.

So many people desire sleep and relief, but choose the numbing drugging option instead of truly addressing the causing issue. It seems easier at first, but in the long term, you not only become addicted to drugs, but you also do not resolve the core issue. The subconscious will seek other ways of getting your attention, and start creating more issues so you can address the core problem and the spiral continues downwards to what seems like an endless pit of avoidance and numbing.

The solution lies in addressing the core problem and recognizing that we need to stop avoiding. Drugs may serve as a temporary solution while addressing the core issue so you can maintain your normal functioning, but make sure it remains very temporary if you have to use it. The core problem is not going away and the longer you avoid it the bigger it seems.

Remember this, it is always smaller than you are. There is no source of anxiousness that is bigger than you, it is part of the illusion. Nothing inside your head, or heart is bigger than you; bigger than your entire being and remember anxiety lives in your ego which is only a part of you, and definitely smaller than what you are capable of overcoming.

Deep sleep and rest is a necessity and your right as a human being, don't take it as optional. The reason that anxiousness or nervousness shows up in sleep is that the subconscious recognizes that you have completed your daily duties and now it has the time to deal with what truly matters. Recognize this as an alarm system that reminds you that you need to address something here, even if it is not fully clear, and it needs to be addressed right then and there, or as soon as possible.

Use sleep is an indicator to how well you are doing or not. See sleeplessness, or restlessness at night as a sign, and thank it for what it is trying to teach you, alerting you that something is not fully processed inside. Something is not integrating and needs addressing with enormous love and kindness towards yourself. Do not be upset or frustrated with yourself, be kind, be gentle, be accepting.

Dedicate some time during the wakeful hours to address those issues and you will gain sounder sleep. Do not let those issues linger, since the lack of sleep will keep you even more fatigued, exhausted, and reactionary. The solution will not come when you start sleeping better, but the other way around. The sooner you deal and address the issue at hand, learn to clear yourself before sleep. You will start to sleep better.

<u>There are a few tips that will help you create a better sleeping atmosphere:</u>

1. Give yourself time to think and contemplate throughout the day or evening. Keeping yourself busy, is an avoidance strategy that doesn't serve you well. TV can wait a little, just be with yourself.

2. Start your sleep routine at least 45 minutes before actually sleeping. Slowing down will ease your brain into slower brain wave patterns. Read a calming book, reduce lighting and TV as it indicates to the brain that it is time for sleep.

3. Write down anything you need to remember for the next day, don't try to remember it because it will keep you alert and trying to remember instead of truly relaxing. You can also keep a small pad and pen by your bedside, just in case you need to write something down.

4. Bedtime is not judging time. It is not a good time to start analyzing your day and what you didn't accomplish. This will only bring you down. Instead, allow yourself to blow away all the stress in imaginary balloons that drift away from you. Allow a quick review of all the joyful moments you experienced that day, and set your intention to have a good day tomorrow. The details are not important at this point of your night; just intend to have a good day tomorrow.

5. Listen to relaxing sleep CDs or read an inspirational book that brings you up. Avoid crime dramas and other negative or thrilling suspense, it will make it more difficult to relax.

There is so much more about creating a better sleeping environment both around you and inside of you. You can watch a complete workshop video I did on my website that includes a guided relaxation as well, at www.lifeachieved.com.

I love it when I hear my clients report they slept like a baby the night following a session, and sleep better overall from that point on. It is truly rewarding to see people looking more rested and peaceful as we continue working together. You, too, deserve to have a restful sound sleep.

Shifting the Heart

No matter what happens in life, if the heart
is suffering you cannot be happy.

We intuitively know how important the heart is. It is the focal point of our most powerful force and the most powerful force in the universe, LOVE. Healing the heart is essential for your well-being and growth. If you are anxious, your heart center suffers.

Anxiety causes havoc in the heart center, and it must be addressed in order to move forward into healing. People with anxiety, learn to cage their heart in order to control it. Bottling up those unpleasant feelings and waiting for them to dissipate with time, hopefully.

Often I hear clients complain of a lump in their chest that just doesn't go away. They feel joyous when it is released. It is beautiful to see how happy they are the first time it happens. The relief in their eyes is priceless. It does not mean the tightness never comes back. But it is different now, they know that they can release it from their body. No need for endless suffering with a deep sense of helplessness. It is possible to release, it is curable, it can shift.

Heart aches are mostly caused by relationships, either with yourself or others. Loved ones, relatives, or people we interact with often, such as, co-workers, bosses, and extended family. There are many other reasons why this tightness in the chest exists, but most of it is about relationships and unresolved challenges in them.

It is important to understand who is triggering the anxiety within you. They don't cause you the anxiety, it is actually your reaction to them. In many cases you can heal yourself out of anxiety without ever changing anything other than your inner perception of the relationship with that particular person. However, sometimes a change must take place. Let me give you some examples.

Dina is a very successful business woman. Type A personality, that usually gets what she wants, in a healthy positive way. Her main concern though was her young adult son, who was struggling with a terrible addiction to drugs. This was devastating her. She feared his death every moment of every day. She dreaded hearing more bad news. She was becoming exceptionally anxious. She dreaded even seeing his phone number when the phone rang. It literally caused her a cringe in her heart. It started disrupting every area in her life. Suddenly, it became hard to function, or go to work. Whenever he was good she was OK, when he was down she was down as well. A roller coaster that was completely outside her control.

We worked diligently at releasing many of these triggers and shifting her perspective and role in their relationship. Her interaction with her son improved dramatically, and she was able to separate herself more healthily from the rollercoaster of his life, maintain her core wellness while supporting him on his journey. By applying these tools and learning new techniques to deal with this situation, Dina transcended from this toxic relationship to find a source of growth and wisdom.

Every relationship serves a purpose, and is a source of potential inner growth. However, it does not mean that it needs to be kept after the lesson has been learned. Some relationships are toxic and negative. They only bring harm, negativity and anxiety. The lessons must be learned quickly and the relationship achieves its purpose and can be let go of, or transcended to more desired dynamics.

I hear of so many people that have a friend that either intentionally or unintentionally causes great distress, anxiousness or triggers negativity. Learn what the purpose of this relationship is. After you understand the lesson, and absorb the wisdom you need to understand about the relationship, you can come to a clear decision whether this relationship can transcend or has already served its purpose.

This is much more complicated with family. The common sense that derives from what I have written so far claims that there must be a reason why you chose this family and usually there is karma you chose to work on together. In many cases there is great animosity that is unclear where it came from between siblings or parents and children. Much of it is explained through past life relationships and grudges that are carried through lifetimes. However, in some cases your family just served you as an entry point, and really you have very little to do with them.

Trying to maintain some relationship is not necessary, and does not need to involve so much heartache. While in a state of deep connection, one of my clients uncovered that her toxic relationship with her mother was all about letting go and learning to move on. It was much easier for her to start the process of letting go of the emotional charge connected with her mother going back over fifty years.

Before you make the decision which kind your family is, please make sure you do some deeper work, and truly get that information from higher parts within yourself. These answers can only come from your higher self or soul. Don't just listen to your regular brain, which is influenced by the ego, grudge, and emotional baggage. This level of consciousness does not hold the answers, it just holds a list of offenses, and the terribly distracting need to know who was right or wrong.

Shifting the heart comes from the deep knowing that you have power. You are not a victim. You are capable of healing your heart. Some wounds are easier to heal than others, but it is all possible if you allow it. Shifting the heart needs your permission. Otherwise you will hold it in until it makes you sick or carry it to your grave. This is not the purpose of emotions. Your heart needs to be content and open. An open heart is a powerful heart. You do need to learn how to guard it, but you do not guard it by closing it in, caging it or suppressing it. It is the wrong way of doing it. Embrace forgiveness and acceptance as it will release YOU from this cage. You are not doing it as a service for others. I know you might feel they don't deserve your forgiveness for all they have wronged you. But do it as a service for yourself. Anxiety, anger, frustration, and pain will be released from the bottom of your heart, so you can be free.

Self-Love

If you experience anxiety on a regular basis, you simply don't love yourself enough. This is a foundational problem that encompasses all other notions in this book. Without forgiveness and acceptance you cannot love yourself. Loving yourself is a challenge to most of us. However, it is a pillar to progression of your heart.

Most confuse self-love with egotism or narcissism, and that is frowned upon by society, thereby causing many of us to not even dare to consider loving ourselves. However, authentic self-love feels completely different. It does not come from the ego, it is not here to inflate you or bring you a sense of entitlement of any kind, without conditions.

You have heard the expression, "If you don't love yourself, you cannot truly love others" and that is very true, however hard to really feel it may be. Most of you might think, "How can I love myself when I am such a failure?" Or "I am just not good enough so I don't deserve to be loved." The real sin is conditioning your self-love and love of others by certain behavior, performance, or quality of your attributes.

This is a longer process of acceptance and understanding that without self-love, you are doomed to a life of discontent.

Here is something you can do right now to help yourself:

EXERCISE - A Loving Sage.

Take a few deep calming breaths!

Imagine a loving, wise, kind, and gentle and patient sage, male or female. How gently they would treat a young child in their care. Now assume the energy of that loving person. Start viewing your anxious, doubtful, and stressed out you, as the child that is deserving of deep comforting and unconditional acceptance. Take a moment and really enjoy assuming both roles.

Allow yourself to imagine that ageless kind, and patient sage truly caring and loving this child unconditionally. Show the vulnerable child the love and care the sage would have towards this child. It is purely unconditional, pure loving. The way you would treat a child that fell off his/her bike at the side of the road.

What calming reassuring guidance would that loving sage give to the child? Give it a few moments, do it now, and allow this to play through...

This is usually best experienced while guided by someone else, however, you can get a taste of true authentic self-love this way. You deserve it. Take a few more moments and savor the calming effect it has.

Shifting the Mind

"Emancipate yourself from mental slavery."
Bob Marley.

We are very cerebral in our society these days. People spend the majority of their day in their head; while at work, planning their day, week, month, year, absorbing information from all sources of media directly to our head.

It is still the general theme of western society that the best form of you is if you all simply become Vulcan - All reason and no emotion. Although we all love Spock, it is just not who we are. We all would love to refine ourselves, however, it is erroneous to believe that our purpose is to become beings of pure reason.

The problems that arise from it is the wish to resolve everything through our minds. Our brains give us many solutions, but give us much grief, as well, because we can refer to it so often that we lose the ability to work with other tools. It is similar to hitting everything with a hammer because it works really well for so many things. Sometimes we need other things to help us and other tools in order to move forward.

Anxiety will not be resolved from the mental level alone. In fact, it is that feeling that we are losing control of our minds that feels the most like a threat to our wellness because most anxious people are very cerebral and usually bring themselves to much higher levels of speed in their minds elevated by the anxiety. It is the common approach that if I process things faster I will be able to catch up. Suddenly, you feel that you need to focus on everything at once just to get a grip of this whirlwind of stuff that needs to happen, and you are so focused on the internal chaos, you don't even notice that your entire level of anxiousness is rising to alarming rates. You are so busy trying to resolve the mess in your head, and it becomes a catch twenty two. Without noticing, you spend your days trying to manage the whirlwind feeling like you are in one of those cash booths with money flying all around you, and can't seem to catch any of it; you just feel overwhelmed and frustrated with your lack of success.

Another metaphor you might relate to is that of a juggler. At first it's easy to juggle three balls at once, but then more and more get added and you start having the feeling that it is becoming too much, but if you let go, the balls will start falling and you will lose control of the whole thing. You are so caught up with trying to keep the balls up in the air that you forget that they will be best handled one at a time and that dropping them all will allow you to truly address them properly. So let go of those balls in the air. It's not doing you any good to keep them flying. It is an illusion that we can do it, don't buy into it. It will cause you enormous amount of frustration and anxiety.

What happens though if those thoughts become obsessive or compulsive, and you feel like they just take over your head and never let go? It consumes you day and night. Then what?

It is important to move out of the realm of this whirlwind that exists within your head into a more pleasurable place inside your being. A place of wisdom, calm, and understanding.

There is a deeper subconscious shift that can release the obsessive thoughts and that provides deeper perspective on the matter at hand. There is something you can do right now that will help you in dealing with an overactive, over stressed mind.

During many of the exercises I do with my clients I find that mental exercises of clearing the mind, sometimes achieve the reverse effect, and bring even more anxiety and frustration. A common fear that anxious people have as soon as I tell them it is time for the relaxation, is, "What if it doesn't work?" or "I don't want to disappoint him, I don't want to be a lost case, I think I am a lost case, I just can't be helped."

To avoid these constant negative, fear based thoughts I chose to shift away from dealing with the mind in a mental way that might or might not work, and simply move you outside of yourself.

Moving the attention outside of you is one of the most helpful things you can do while anxious. These exercises in the next few chapters will help you to truly see the beauty in them, and outside of you. It will bring you relief from the hamster wheel and move you into peace and perspective.

The Perspective of Empathy

Anxiety derives from you spending too much time in your own head and lacking perspective. Empathy could be a wonderful heart and mind exercise to get you out of your head and shoes and place you in somebody else's shoes. This exercise in perspective will not only help you get out of the anxious mode and into greater emotional understanding, it will also allow you to be more engaged with the people around you in a healthy way.

Empathy is not sympathy. Sympathy is when you agree with someone's opinion or way of thinking and emotion. Empathy is simply placing yourself in their shoes and head, without the need to agree or disagree. Seeing things from their own point of view, and the process of their thinking, as it is right now. The neutrality in this approach will give you freedom from absorbing their energies, or the need to fix their situation, just witness it from their inner world.

For example, when someone is telling you how terrible their relationship is with their partner, you don't have to take their side or agree with them on what they did. You don't need to offer advice either, just try and see it from their point of view. When you do this, you are doing a wonderful job and completely separating from the anxiety of your own situation and from the need to come up with a solution.

Let's say Abby is telling you how terrible Bob is and what he said to her last night. Empathy will draw you to say, "I can see how this would upset you," and not "Wow, he is definitely behaving like an idiot." You don't have to take their position, you can just witness it.

Start witnessing and showing empathy and seeing things from other people's point of view or state of being. When dealing with your children for example, see what made them upset, don't try to solve their problem without acknowledging their feelings first. Otherwise they will feel misunderstood, and you will feel the lack of ability to fix things quickly for them and for yourself.

Now start showing empathy for YOURSELF!

EXERCISE - Empathy for YOURSELF!

Listen to your own story from outside, without committing to it. Observing in a neutral non-judging way. Don't worry about finding the solution, just listen to the story. How the anxiety keeps popping when thinking of this person, situation, trigger. Don't get sucked into your head again, just witness it with pure empathy and acceptance. This exercise will let go of much of your anxiety right on the spot. You will feel lighter and less dense than before. It really is like stepping outside of the dense bubble that this story is in and looking at it from the outside, free and light.

This is not dissociation, or detachment, it is actually a healthy way of not being too hard on yourself. Giving yourself the breather that you need from what you are experiencing in a positive, constructive way. Do not detach, simply observe with love and kindness, with empathy. The point of view is that of a loving grandparent, unconditional love to the youngster within, and if you will notice, the anxious you, is usually very young in character usually between 5-12 years old. Observe yourself and that anxious you with loving, caring eyes, and notice what age is your anxious self.

EXERCISE - Age of Anxious Self.

Close your eyes, take a moment and do this. Observe your anxious self and "feel" how old might it be?

Do you have more empathy and compassion towards the anxious part of you?

Will you treat this part of you with more gentleness?

Is it easier to be more understanding and fatherly/motherly with that part?

I bet it is!

Keep on doing this exercise so you keep the perspective of love and empathy.

Shifting the Soul

You are not a human being with a soul, but
a soul experiencing being human.

The Purpose of Life on Earth

You chose to have a human life. Yes, you chose it. Your soul decided to experience what it is to have emotions in this challenging place called earth. Many lessons can be learned in a short period of time. You chose a theme and several key experiences that will lay a foundation, a blue print for this experience and then...doing it. Using your free will to see how you would do in this journey with the challenges and scenarios you laid out for yourself. It almost always feels harder than anticipated from the other side.

Going through this journey of life is challenging mostly when we do not sense the purpose of things that we experience. Sometimes, that is the point and sometimes it is just unnecessary suffering. So it is our task to start separating and releasing those torments we put on ourselves unnecessarily. It is time to listen to our emotions and the wisdom that is encapsulated in them, so we may grow. Because that is the purpose of life.

The purpose of life is to experience what we came here to experience, learn from it and grow. The purpose of this is the expansion of our soul and source. Through the expansion of our soul we expand our source/ god/ creator. We are the far reaching branches of consciousness seeking the thrill of experience and growth. We are at the leading edge of consciousness.

So there it is, the purpose of life.

Another question comes to mind; why grow and experience a human life? Why would a beautiful soul want to go through this process?

Well, as a soul, when all is peace, joy, and you are connected and balanced, it is unfathomable to experience raw emotions such as pain, suffering or aloneness. Experiences you are completely engrossed in and need to complete. Deep understanding - growth in this super challenging game called life on earth. But this challenge is intricate and has consequences in its actions. This is very stimulating for a soul and only the bravest, and most curious embark on such an adventure. So know this, you are already a courageous, adventurous soul who is thirsty for growth and expansion.

The Purpose of Not Knowing

Some people may wonder why do we still not remember all this? The answer is remarkably simple and I will give some examples.

Would you enjoy a movie if someone had already told you the plot and the surprise ending?

I don't think so, you will not enjoy it half as much and definitely be even slightly bored. Let's take another example.

Imagine you are going through one of those mazes, like a corn maze. Why do you do it? Usually to have fun and challenge yourself. Will you end up in the same place eventually? Yes, but you will gain an enriching experience. If you walked in with a map, without any chances of taking the wrong turn, as ropes guide you through the correct path, would you feel excited? Absolutely not!

Will it evoke the same level of emotions? No, it will actually be rather boring and unsatisfying, and you would not have that little thrill, fun, sense of adventure, and the "risk" of getting lost, that you were seeking in the first place. So, not knowing, not having the map, but feeling your way through it is the true essence of the experience. It is what gives it our chance to fully engage and figure out how to solve challenges, setbacks, and making successes that much sweeter and rewarding.

We like to do this often in our life because we enjoy it. We play video games trying to figure out how to complete levels and move on to a more challenging one. We go hiking on new trails, so we can return home with another satisfying experience under our belt. Some of these hikes are challenging, and may require more effort that you anticipated. But those are the ones we remember the most, along with connecting with nature and experiencing those beautiful views that made it all worthwhile. Do you get the same enjoyment from looking at a picture of that place? It is enjoyable, but not nearly as much seeing and experiencing it fully by being there yourself.

Many people ask me why are we not allowed to know more of our purpose and direction in life, and the answer is a little more complicated than that. Most people feel desperate and just want the cheat sheet for life. They want that map for the maze, that rope that will help them out of a situation. But it does not work that way, you have to learn it through experience. However, you can get some guidance and direction along the way just to help you know that you are on the right path. Hints and tips that will assist, but not solve it fully for you. Stop worrying, stressing out, and getting filled with anxiety because you do not know. You can get some guidance, but you are the one that still has to solve the puzzle, and come out feeling triumphant at the end. Even if you do not see it right now.

So here we are, ready to embrace the experience, feel the emotions, and live, learn and grow from the experience. But why does it have to be so hard? Why do we have to hold on to all this anxiety and pain, and keep reliving it?

We don't!

That is a mistake that we do while disconnected from our greater selves. Once we experience what we are here to experience, learn and grow, we can release it. There is no need to continue suffering. We need to let go - once we learn the wisdom that awaits. Our emotions are encapsulating enormous wisdom within them and it is our task to understand and gain that wisdom so we may grow, and expand, and release what is not needed anymore.

Soul Healing

So let's begin our journey to spiritual-emotional wisdom and expansion.

It is time to acknowledge our greater reality. We have reached a point in our human existence and development in which we need to recognize that we are more than what we seem in our three dimensional world. I am not here to tell you what to believe, or what not to believe. However, after working with hundreds of people from diverse backgrounds, nationalities, religious beliefs or the lack of them, I have come to realize there is a greater common thread to all of us. I will dedicate a separate book for this endeavor because it is so big and encompassing to our human experience. I will merely scrape the surface with some truths. You may choose to accept them now, or later in life, or after you transition. At some point you will accept this, because it is the basis of who we are.

We are greater beings living a human life!

Whether you would like to call it consciousness, or soul, or anything else that you are comfortable using, that larger part of who you are, it is essential for our existence because it is the basis of who we are, pure energy, pure consciousness that never ceases to exist, it simply grows further and further with each experience.

I like to use concepts that are clean of any influence of a particular religion or movement of thought for we have a certain charge when we hear words that represent something our conscious mind approves of or disapproves. In short, I will use words such as pure consciousness or an energy that is pure consciousness, to represent what we usually hear as our soul.

We do not come as a "clean slate" to this world. We are a combination of nature and nurture and more. We inherent trauma through our genes, we inherent certain characteristics and tendencies in our DNA. However, not many consider that our soul comes with unresolved trauma or anxiety from previous experiences. We come again to resolve, heal, and transcend those anxieties, and previous emotions from the souls past.

Our anxieties may be sourced from our experiences, ancestry, personality, or our soul. This is why you need to consider the full spectrum of healing. It is true that anxieties are triggered in this life you are experiencing, now. However, at times, something that is triggered by a current life event goes far beyond the specific event you have experienced, now, and is rooted deeper in your soul's past.

A few years ago I had a client, let's call her Sarah. She came to me for several different reasons and clarity she was seeking. In one of these sessions, she mentioned something that was rather silly, yet embarrassing to her. She has this remarkable "talent" to faint every time she visits a loved one in the hospital. In fact, these fainting spells were getting to be expected by the extended family. She wanted to find out why is this happening, and if we could release it.

I took her through the relaxation and visualization that would lead her to the core of this issue in her subconscious. We explored current life events and recognized that none of them were the source of this issue. So we went on to explore other lives. She then became very emotional, I calmed her gently and she relaxed back very quickly. She said, "One hundred and one. I had to bury one hundred and one of them." As we explored the scene further, she described that her village was ransacked and pillaged by a Roman legion that went through and killed everyone in the village. They left a few alive to bury the dead, and then killed them, as well. She went through the horrific ordeal of burying her entire family, relatives, neighbors and all the people she knew in that small village.

We then brought the deeper wisdom and understanding of how it relates to her now. Since that event, she has been carrying that horrible fear of losing her loved ones every time she saw them in situations that even remotely reminded her of their possible death (being in the hospital). She could not handle it again and preferred not dealing with it rather than suffer again. The subconscious chose to check-out by fainting, losing consciousness. We spent a few more moments releasing, healing, and learning everything we could from that life.

She emailed me four days later and told me that our session was tested sooner than she expected. She needed to take her mother to some tests in the hospital, and to her great relief, she did not faint, she in fact did not have any problem at all, no anxiousness whatsoever, and definitely no fainting. She is still very committed to her extended family, but now it is done with less fear and more motherly care. Sarah healed herself from a trauma she would never would have guessed took place close to two thousand years ago.

The soul sometimes waits for the right opportunity to heal something. It can all be done in the in between lives period of healing. However, sometimes we chose to heal it through experience. We can heal so much of our karmic cycles and soul's wounds. It is remarkably easy to do in the right state, when you are ready on all levels of your being. Transcending pain to a higher understanding and wisdom.

Dealing with your soul's past lives is not only for resolving trauma and hurt. It can serve you by empowering you and reminding you of your Strength and possibilities.

I recently had a session with Kayla, and she had much confusion, doubt and anxiousness on where to take her life. We did some past lives exploration and she witnessed a life as a Native American medicine woman who was gifted with herbs and plants, healing many people in her life. We witnessed several more scenes that were important for other reasons, as well. We visited another life as a young knight who became a powerful warrior and was very close to his king and did good service to him. He started a family, which was well taken care of. He lived and died by the sword at age twenty five.

These two lives were filled with dignity, power, and independence. We asked her higher self some other questions and healing, and asked for the purpose of showing us these two lives. Very clearly she received the knowing that she is a powerful healer and a warrior. She needs to remember this now and apply it to this life. Bring those qualities back. She has all this power stored in her, it just needs to be remembered and unleashed. Needless to say she felt really good, and empowered at the end of this session. She sent me an email several days later, thanking me for my assistance, and telling me how she had made her decision with the power and clarity she needed.

Work on the soul level is fascinating and powerful. Much can be accomplished, and it always addresses a very relevant predicament or something you need right now to live THIS life in a better and fuller way.

What is your soul trying to tell you?

PHASE THREE

Returning to Power

Reclaiming Your Personal Power

The most important thing you need to know is that this power already exists within you. Never look for it in other people, places or the next big thing. It has always, and will always, come from within! Just as we have seen with Kayla in the previous chapter.

You sometimes accidentally give your power away to fear and anxiety, but it is only temporary. Now that you are aware of it, your power is naturally drawn back to you. You are not allowing these accidental drains of energy to take place.

Imagine yourself as a power plant of life force. It is important not to have any unnecessary drains on your energy system. All stress and anxiety is stealing your energy, your power; your force-field weakens when you let your mind wander in those directions. Just by knowing this you start managing your power plant better, recognizing quicker what drains you and what recharges you.

The recharging of this life force comes from reconnecting with the universe and your soul. Exactly like plugging your phone to the charger. Imagine there is a source of energy a foot above your head, and just like regular electricity when you are stressed or anxious you cause resistance in the system and the energy gets lost before you even get charged. Or even worse, not allowing yourself to recharge properly, feeling drained. So let it flow. When you let go of things, you allow that life force to flow through you. This is basic science; we are energy.

Three things need to happen in order to allow the energy to flow:

1. Open the channels that replenish you, and keep them open.
2. Reduce resistance - no open anxieties, fear or pain that drains the energy.
3. Get recharged daily - activate your power source through meditations, enriching activities, gratitude, exercise, and LOVE to yourself and others.

Start treating yourself as an energy system and very quickly you will start recognizing who and what fills you up, and who and what is draining. What role they play in your life.

Activating your power source

Reclaiming your power is not a single event in time and space, it is a series of understanding and actions you initiate. There is a major shift that takes place in the understanding of your greater reality of who you are as a person, remembering how much power you have over your life.

You might remember that at some point in your life you felt well, happy, flowing. Some of us might need to go back to childhood in order to remember how that felt. I like to regress my clients to a really good memory, and remind them how wonderful it felt to be this way. Some people don't even have that, and I have to go into past lives to show them that they were happy at some point in their history as a soul. Being in that deeper trance state allows you to bring it back without the clutter of the mundane brain and ego.

You activate it!

Move away from the bogged trenches you fell into and realize your greatness.

In the program, I go deeper into exercises and personal activation of power. There is much you can do by embracing concepts and exercises that will bring a shift within. Bringing you closer and closer towards personal power.

Authentic personal power is: peace, calm, and confidence, meaning, and purpose. It is not ego driven and inflated. It is inspired by wellness and flow.

The sense of power is feeling Mastery over life.

It does not mean there are no challenges, but it means you are feeling capable and know that this challenge is serving a purpose even if it eludes you at this point. Knowing that it is placed in your life for a reason, and the reason is never to make you suffer, but to understand that there is a lesson and potential for personal growth behind everything. That little things do not need to bother you.

Take the time in the next few pages and really do the exercises fully. Notice how different you feel afterwards. Notice the beauty in things around you, and in recognizing a greater perspective.

The Power of Forgiveness & Acceptance

Acceptance is the birth of liberation from anxiety.

Acceptance is the key segment to this whole program, because acceptance is done out of your own power and intention. It is the deeper understanding of the greater picture and your proper place in it. Acceptance does not mean surrender, it means understanding things as they are.

Surrender means giving up, especially to the power of others or other forces. It is the yielding of oneself to the whims of others, with a sense of defeat and disempowerment. However, acceptance brings a receiving, a welcoming into a group, finding yourself suitable and being accepted. This act of accepting is most powerful when done by you and of you. Accepting yourself into the exclusive club of you. You give yourself permission to be you, in the highest, purest way; not allowing yourself to degenerate and be mean to others and do as you please regardless of others' well-being, but being tolerant of your own delicate parts of your heart and soul. My favorite acceptance statement is:

"It is Okay to be me."

Say it now, at least five times and notice the reverberation it creates within you.

When you do not accept things as they are, you suffer greatly, and that is most of the suffering you are experiencing. You do not accept your own vulnerability, you do not accept others as they are, you do not see the world in an objective manner so, in other words, acceptance is the birth of expanded awareness. The awareness and perspective that you provide yourself on anything and everything.

Acceptance releases the shackles of anxiety from your energy system. Accepting that things can be different, life does not have to be this way. It is like having Harry Houdini on your side untangling you completely out of something you thought could not be untangled. The liberation is profound since you are truly releasing yourself on so many levels, and energetically, it is the most important work. It is the energy of entanglement that places your thought in the captivity of anxiousness and constricts your body and your muscles from allowing the natural flow of things. Therefore, bringing the dis-ease the body feels, not allowing the body to receive the natural flow.

Acceptance is the main ingredient in the liberation of your soul from the binds of anxiety.

Many people enter my office completely engulfed in their anxiousness. Measuring their wellness by how bad the anxiety was throughout the week. They are so skewed that they cannot see the world in any other way, it is all consuming and exhausting. At that point it, is the frustration they experience about themselves, not accepting self, filled with the self-judgment, frustration, anger, and expectations that perpetuate the cycle of non-acceptance.

So how do you do it?

A client just told me yesterday that working with the subconscious has shifted him completely in ways that he could not achieve otherwise. He intellectually knew how he is supposed to view the world, but could not integrate it to his entire being and really feel and think this way. The deeper work with the subconscious and soul level brought this change and helped create the shift he needed to really operate from that space of acceptance and compassion that he had sought previously and could not grasp.

Listen to the meditations and self-hypnosis recordings I have made for this program, as they will truly help you shift on a deeper level. This is not a simple re-programming of the brain as some might describe it. It will shift your energetic body, physical body, and release you from the karmic cycle you have gathered in other lives, as well. It is a re-patterning of your own energies, and everything is energy. Our thoughts and emotions are simply at the forefront of the "true experiencer", your soul. Some call it inner-being, consciousness. Please accept that it is part of your greater self, whatever you are comfortable calling it based on your current perception and belief system.

The process of acceptance is quite personal and requires your full intent in creating it. Acceptance is the process of bringing unconditional love into the situation. Sprinkle in plenty of forgiveness and kindness and it will start tasting more and more like freedom and liberation from anxiety.

Let's try and get more intimate with the feelings of forgiveness and acceptance.

It is true that the overwhelming emotion is fear, but there are many others that need to be addressed in order to bring healing and reconciliation within.

It is hard to pinpoint when you first think of the events that bring anxiety, but there is plenty of blame: judgment, frustration, and disappointment in ourselves when thinking of this anxiety.

I know that when I say this you will feel the resistance within you to forgiving yourself for what happened or accepting it as an event. But it is time to acknowledge it and be KIND to yourself.

You may ask, "What am I forgiving myself for?"

Forgiving self for allowing this to happen, for becoming vulnerable at the wrong time, in front of others, for feeling fear when I know it is misplaced. These are all harsh judgments of self that come from the EGO. "What will they say if they knew I am having a panic attack?" "They will think I am weak, that I cannot handle it, they will see me for who I really am, I might die, I will lose control...." and on and on and on.

Release yourself from this pre-built judgment system that right now is actually causing the fear of anxiety attack, and the fear that it might happen anywhere - while I'm driving, while I'm at a meeting, while presenting, while I am alone and there will be no one to help me.

Forgive yourself that it happened, forgive yourself that it might happen, forgive yourself that it is happening - It's OK.

Here is a good affirmation to address this issue, and we will do it also in the self-hypnosis recording that will help you integrate it deeper inside your subconscious. So let's do it now.

EXERCISE: Forgiveness and Acceptance.

Feel that these words have power to release it from inside your body, really feel them flowing out right as you say them. Feel the power of your words and conviction. Take a moment after each statement and allow it to take place.

Take a deep breath, release your breath very slowly, close your eyes and say:

"I release myself from all negative judgments!"

Take another slow breath and say:

"I fully and wholly forgive myself for experiencing anxiety!"

Another slow breath and say:

"I fully and wholly accept myself and know deep inside that it is OK to be me!"

I already know that at this point it might be hard for you to truly believe it, and you have just realized how much you were judging yourself. It is key to repeat these statements at least once a day. Like all other affirmations, you will do in this book, they are vital to the change that you desire. They are one of the most powerful tools you have to create the shift you desire - Use them!

The repetition will open the possibility to creating a new belief system.

Take the time now and process this new approach and reflect on how much you have not accepted or forgiven yourself, and you will notice the liberation that comes from doing so!

The Power of Words

"Be impeccable with your words."
Don Miguel Ruiz

Words, emotions, and thoughts have enormous power over our body, heart, and mind. There is now scientific proof to the matter that words have energy and it is influencing us all the time. Quantum Physics reiterates that everything is energy and we must apply this concept not just for the physical world, but to our own ecosystem of emotions, thoughts, and words. Everything has a certain vibration, positive or negative, and we can consciously start choosing what we want to be. We have the power to consciously move ourselves from words of negativity, anxiety, and distress to words of power and positivity. It has enormous effect on us on the cellular level and I wish to bring a couple of important research example in this matter.

In his book *Messages in Water*, Dr. Masaru Emoto, applied the scientific method into his research on how water molecules react to human consciousness. I highly recommend reading more about his comprehensive research in this area. In some of his experiments that were repeated all over the world, he took containers of water and spoke to them every day. To some he had said "thank you" and to others he said "you fool." Upon freezing the water he could clearly observe how beautiful and complete the water molecules that were told "thank you" were. The pictures of the frozen water molecules that were told "you fool," were visibly distorted and incomplete.

These experiments continued for many years with many different words such as love, hate, hope, etc. At some point he decided to see if the words themselves without the human speech would have that power over the water and he did a double blind experiment in which he had his students place covered labels of words on the vial of water and not interact with them at all. He tested them and found that simply the word itself had the power to distort or perfect the water molecules that were observed. It is remarkable to think that a printed word has such power on its environment. Everything is energy and it reflects the consciousness behind it and influences its environment in a powerful way.

Why is it important to you and me?

WE ARE SEVENTY PERCENT WATER!

Those words, even printed ones, have power to influence US on the cellular level. Be mindful. This is further proof that words, emotions, and thoughts are all energy, and vibrate on different levels based on what you think, say, hear, or feel. We are not swimming in an ocean of energy, we ARE part of it. We are a conscious concentration of energy within energy.

All of this influences our environment and ourselves with serious ramifications. It influences our health. If the water gets distorted, everything with water in it, in our body, will get slightly distorted, as well. With time, it may bring enormous consequence to the health of our cells and entire systems.

It is vital to explore what language you use on a regular basis, what do you say to others and yourself? What words do you say to yourself, what you feel? Do you say, "I am such a fool...", or "I hate my life?" etc. Stop yourself from continuing the self-pollution of your own sacred waters.

The power of words received further studying and measuring. Sir David R. Hawkins, M.D., Ph.D. created a map of consciousness in his book, *Power-Vs-Force*. He measured emotions and concepts, and placed them on a scale from zero to one thousand. Through kinesiology, he tested on what level of energy they vibrate. Here is a portion of his map and just a speck of his expansive research in the field of consciousness, I highly recommend you read his material:

Map of Consciousness :

Level Log/Calibration Emotion

Enlightenment 700 - 1,000 Pure Consciousness

Peace 600 Illumination

Joy 540 Serenity

Love 500 Reverence

Reason 400 Understanding

Acceptance 350 Forgiveness

Willingness 310 Optimism

Neutrality 250 Trust

Courage 200 Affirmation

The above are levels of Truth

The below are levels of falsehood

Pride 175 Scorn

Antagonistic 150 Hate

Desire 125 Lust

Fear 100 Anxiety

Grief 75 Regret

Apathy/Hatred 50 Despair

Guilt 30 Blame

Shame 20 Humiliation

*Excerpt from the book Power vs. Force by David R. Hawkins, M.D., Ph.D.

It is interesting to notice that below two hundred are negative levels that move you away from your truth. As you can see, anxiety and fear at level one hundred, is a vibration of falsehood. It is not real, it is moving you away from who you are. It moves your thoughts and emotions to lower energetic levels that make you feel dense, disconnected, and limit the flow of life and truth.

Let us see how it affects us in our daily reality. When you say, "I hate...." you bring that level of energy into your system, into every cell of your body. When you think, "I suck at..." you bring that reality into your mind, body, and heart. When you think, "I am always anxious," you are causing reverberations of anxiety through your body, along with committing it into your belief system about yourself.

Since everything is energy, you can do a conscious choice to start shifting into higher levels of consciousness and being. This is the way to free yourself from anxiety; lifting yourself away from the cycles of fear and anxiousness into levels that are free of them. When you feel trust (250 on the scale) you are completely away from anxiousness (100 on the scale). When you feel trust, you are feeling the vibration of trust and cannot feel anxiousness at that moment. That is the key. When you move up the scale above 200, at that moment in time you cannot feel those lower vibration feelings that shift your entire outlook and perspective on life.

We, of course, fluctuate between many feelings on that scale, but know that you can reduce that extreme fluctuation by choosing a more conscious approach to managing the words and thoughts you are producing. At first you will be worried, "I'm thinking too many negative thoughts," but remember that awareness is the first step to any change. Continuous practice in choosing words and thoughts will move your mind to different places. This is a process, don't expect perfection within a week. However, you will start to be more careful with what you think, say, and bring onto yourself and others. Your mind will start to feel more manageable than before.

Start shifting your thoughts into possibilities, and openness and leave fatalism and bleakness behind you. Shift your mind to accepting that the only thing that is constant is change, and you can change your mind, change your thoughts, and change your life for the better.

Let go of the idea that you will always be anxious, and start shifting it towards the idea that you are moving towards peace, right now, with every word that your read. Your natural state of being, is peace. The anxiousness and stress are false, they are tacked-on mistakenly, and can be shifted.

You will always fluctuate on that scale of consciousness, but know that you can always reach for longer durations on the higher levels and graceful, short, lows. Now, it is more fluid and tangible than you have thought previously.

I knew I really got it when I stopped saying the f... word. Because I knew that it does not serve me. I no longer send judging thoughts to others so carelessly because it reduces my own energy. I am not perfect, but I am miles away from where I was ten or fifteen years ago. I used to know the negative power of words and my sharp mind, by shooting poison arrows towards people that I wanted to put down at work. I could visibly see the hurt I caused to some, and that was all driven by ego and a false sense of power. There was no glory in it, simply hurt.

Now I am a lot more careful with my tongue and notice that I think completely differently about others. I simply see that their world view is vibrating at those lower emotions that are tainting their heart and minds. I do not judge them for it, it is simply where they are in this moment in time. If they want my help, I would love to assist them in the process of moving to higher vibration, but they need to do the work if they want permanent change.

Use the power of your words for truth and love. Think first, "Is what I am about to say going to bring the person up? Can I rephrase it? Would it increase their awareness or will it just put them down?"

Don't expect perfection, just be conscious, and choose positive words that are open and expansive. Don't lash out and shoot poison arrows of negatively charged emotions, they will not serve you or the other person in any way, not now, and not in the future.

Make sure you are also not stuck in just desiring higher vibration, it is another trap that will keep you lower in that scale.

When you desire something don't say, "I want to be calm" because it will only emphasize the inner knowing that you want it, but do not have it, raising frustration. Instead say "I am calm."

When you start saying things in the present tense you will start bringing that vibration into your consciousness faster than you think.

Instead of saying, "I want to be at peace." You can say this powerful statement, "I am at peace." Say it and notice the immediate shift.

You may say, "I am calm," "I am free," "I am."

Take a deep breath and think of how you want to be, as if you already are, and state it!

The Power of the Law of Attraction

Much has been written about the law of attraction, and as a person who has used it and taught workshops on it for many years, I can sum it up very easily and teach you how to do it right.

1. Basic physics - Like attracts like. A drop of water will be attracted to another drop of water that is nearby because they are the same. In order to attract that which you want (peace, calm, confidence) you need to have the essence, the energy of that, in order to attract more of it from the universe around you.
2. Become the essence of that which you dream to be. In other words, Imagine it - feel it - it will become your reality.

Let me explain it in more detail. Do not fall for the "fake it until you make it" attitude because inside you will know it is fake, and, therefore, not believable or effective. Saying an affirmation without really believing or feeling it is an absolute waste of time.

It is about the vibe of how it REALLY feels that will bring you the essence of that which you want, thereby making it your reality.

What is important, is to bring the feeling and essence of how it feels when you have it. Create the right vibration and energy and it becomes your reality. When you feel the essence of calm and peace, you will be calm and peaceful. Even if it is only for a moment. The more you spend time in that essence, the more you will attract it into your life as you are vibrating in that energy pattern. Only then will you be truly attracting it like a magnet into your life.

Let's do a quick exercise to really bring it home.

EXERCISE: Stepping Into the Right Essence.

Step 1 - Take a deep slow breath and even slower exhale and know that you are ready to begin.

Step 2- Use your vivid imagination (remember you have a good one because you can imagine fear and anxiety really well). Bring within your mind the ultimate image of how you want to FEEL, whether it's calm, confident, balanced, at peace, strong, relaxed, free to do activities that you would love to do, etc.

Step 3 - It can take the form of anything you want; a super hero, an animal spirit, a super you, a character from a movie, a book, or a completely fantastic creature, a phoenix, an elf, a wizard, don't be shy, let your mind go to that ideal essence that will symbolize it for you in the best way possible. Take a moment and find it.

Step 4 - Imagine that perfect symbol is a step in front of you and make it as real as possible. Especially focus on how it feels more than anything else.

Step 5 - Now, take a deep breath and step into that essence with one step forward, and breathe it in, feel as if it is soaking through your skin and mind, immerse in it. Take your time, really FEEL it. Let it shift your heart and body, notice how much more relaxed you feel in it. How it loosens old patterns and melts them out of you easily.

Step 6 - Be that super you, and bring it with you from now on. Allow your muscle memory to remember how it feels to be in this essence. Take a few moments and allow it to really change your attitude, feeling, and reality. Notice how different it is to view the world from those eyes. It is even easier since you are becoming one with that essence.

The Power of Statements & Affirmations

Affirmations and statements are powerful tools of change. An effective healer will equip you with relevant affirmations. It is important that you apply the law of attraction when saying these affirmations as described in the previous chapter, otherwise they will be less effective. I like to take it a step further and move into statements. What is the difference between affirmations and statements? It might be semantics to some, but when you hear the word statement, you hear power. An affirmation seems a little weaker to me, at least this is how I feel about it. A statement declares truth to the world, in a clear and powerful way. Therefore, even if it is not truth, yet, as soon as it is said, it becomes truth, it becomes your reality. So I like to call them statements, they feel even more powerful than affirmations.

In all honesty, when I first started working on affirmations and gratitude the idea of it seemed rather silly to me. A lot of the self-help books take a very basic approach and they don't dedicate enough time to the concept of why it is important. A "just do it, it's great" approach. But I got over it when I gave it proper attention and realized how powerful and immediate the effect is on me.

Statements are most effective if you resonate with them completely. I encourage you to take the ones I will provide you throughout this book and see if they resonate with you. Some will be intentionally stretching your comfort zone, but others will simply be not specific enough to your particular challenge, and will need some adjustment. You can do those adjustments, however, you need to follow some basic guidelines for writing a good powerful statement.

EXERCISE: Powerful Statements Need Three Main Ingredients:

---

1. It really means something to YOU, it resonates with you.

Make it inspiring and touching, something that moves you from the inside such as freedom from anxiety and stress. The desire for inner calm and peace.

2. It is positive, focusing on what you want to move towards, not on what you are moving away from, or wish to avoid.

Avoid saying, "I want to be free of stress and anxiety."

Move to, "I want to be calm and at peace." (We are not done yet)

3. It is in the current moment, in the NOW, not in future tense.

Avoid saying "I want..." it will only frustrate you, because you don't have it, yet.

Move to "I **am** calm and at peace." Having it right NOW!

Now it is complete. It vibrates on a higher frequency of wellness. I can feel it right away when I say it, and you intuitively recognize it, as well.

4. Continue the process of refinement for your statement.

So here are a few more examples you might like to work with:

+ I Feel Safe and comfortable in my environment.
+ I am calm. I am peace.
+ I am connected with my inner being and the universe.
+ Every day, in every way, I am getting better and better.
+ It's okay to be me.
+ I am cool, calm, and collected.
+ I love myself deeply and unconditionally.
+ I create positive thoughts and feelings of wellness.
+ I am safe. I am protected.
+ I enjoy life and its mysteries.
+ There is wisdom and growth in everything.
+ I am powerful beyond my imagination.

The Power of Gratitude

In a recent study, it has been proven scientifically that people who use gratitude are twenty five percent happier than those who do not. So let's take a more serious look at gratitude.

You might feel intellectually that it will probably not help you much, if at all, and it might be true in your experience when you dedicated a few fleeting seconds to gratitude, and it didn't make a big impact, however you are mistaken. I have never witnessed a moment with a client or myself, when truly dedicating five minutes to flood yourself with gratitude, did not result in feeling better. You will always feel better, and definitely will climb to a freer emotion on the scale of wellness. It will happen, just give it the time.

The challenge feels greater when you are stuck in anxiousness, stress or that overwhelming sense that you really can't do anything. At that moment it is hard to get the emotion of gratitude towards anything. You are too consumed by the anxiety and feel as if it is going to take over. However, there is a beautiful exercise that will show you how easy it is to shift yourself intentionally. The more you practice it, the easier it gets, and the easier you can shift.

There is a higher cosmic explanation of why it is so powerful; with gratitude comes grace, and grace brings very high vibration. When you are in a higher vibration you will not have stress and anxiousness, it does not exist on this energy level. It goes even deeper than that. Gratitude is the recognition of source and the gifts you have received directly from God/universe/source. It is the thank you, that you hear after giving a gift and feel "it was all worth it, you are welcome." This sense of elation is felt reverberating across the universe every time you acknowledge the gifts you were given. Saying Thank you, raises the vibration of the giver. No matter what is given or received, a thank you always feels good. The universe will feel this higher vibration and will send you more of the same vibration in your direction, as the law of gravity and attraction works continuously on all your think, say, do, and feel.

So by practicing gratitude, you begin ripples of higher, freer energy in your life and around the world.

Now that you understand it more fully, why would you not do that?

There are numerous exercises you can do, and they don't require an enormous amount of time, simply your conscious intention.

EXERCISE - How to Gain Profound Gratitude in Two Words

A few years ago I saw the movie *The Shift* by Dr. Wayne Dyer, and I loved it. One of the jewels I learned from Wayne was that when he wakes up in the morning, he simply says, "Thank you!" and that opens deep appreciation and gratitude in him for the rest of the day. Wow, I thought, that is profound. When I started practicing saying it in the morning, with the full understanding of its implications, I could only smile and be deeply grateful for this life. Saying a simply **thank you - every morning** encompasses all of this for me:

Thank you for giving me another day on this magnificent planet.

Thank you for the opportunity to make a difference in people's lives,

Thank you for what I am learning from life,

Thank you for my family that I love so dearly,

Thank you for my body that serves me and I need to respect more,

Thank you for showing me beauty outside my window and in my heart,

Thank you for the lessons and growth I experience,

Thank you for experiencing emotions,

Thank you for enriching my soul with this life,

Thank you for showing me my unique path,

Thank you for tasty food,

Thank you for the taste buds that allow me to enjoy food,

Thank you for the air I breathe,

Thank you for Swiss chocolate,

Thank you for my comfortable bed,

Thank you for my cat that brings me so much joy,

Thank you for colors and eye sight to enjoy them,

Thank you for my silliness and humor,

Etc., etc.

The list can go on and on, and please don't stop even in the smallest and silliest of things, the longer the list, the more time you spend in gratitude, the better you will feel at the end of it. Who do I thank? It doesn't matter, you can pick whomever or whatever suits you, just open that channel and be thankful!

So start your own journal of gratitude and fill it every day, or just type it on your computer and start a file of daily gratitude on your desktop, or start saying thank you when you wake up in the morning.

And remember that when I say thank you it goes deep, and I want to send ripples of light and wellness to the entire universe because I know how powerful it is, so...

Thank You!

EXERCISE - Spontaneous Appreciation of Beauty.

The point of this exercise is to take any moment in life and look around you with eyes of wonderment at the beauty and specialness of things around you - appreciating things by allowing us to step for a moment, outside of our silly mundane brain.

Here is an example I like to give in many of my workshops:

You are stuck in traffic and this might cause you discomfort or worse a source of anxiety. You start thinking of how annoyed you are and your emotional state starts to deteriorate. Take a deep breath and allow yourself to disconnect from that mundane brain and open your eyes as if you are seeing things for the first time with that sense of wonderment children have. Shift and start the process of appreciation:

Realizing you are driving in a large machine filled with computers that is exceptionally comfortable, how amazed would your ancestors be, seeing you in this technological marvel, gliding effortlessly with a touch of your leg and hand, controlling this machine, controlling the temperature inside, listening to music, having a conversation with your loved ones miles away, sometimes even having a conversation with people across the world over unseen waves of energy. How remarkable is that? Riding in this marvelous machine that can travel at high speeds without any effort of yours. You would seem to be like an astronaut to them. What lovely lines and contours the design of the car has, it is quite pleasing to the eye. How beautiful is that building, tree you just went by...

Example 2 - You are standing in line...shift and start noticing the design of things. Notice the shapes of the decorations, the structure of the building. You notice the shapes of things and how some of them are designed to be very pleasing and attract your attention, how beautiful they are. How pleasing the combination of colors are on an ad, or shelf...

Example 3 - When was the last time you truly took a moment to realize the immensity and magic of a tree. I remember the first time I felt that trees have consciousness, that they are aware of their interaction with nature around them.

You move from ordinary perception of reality to extra-ordinary view of things, appreciating them and the remarkable ingenuity that brought them about. Notice art, architecture, how beautiful is that piece of furniture.

When you start focusing and appreciate the beauty that is always around you, you will gain perspective on things. Gaining perspective is half the battle with anxiety, we no longer focus on it, and we give ourselves the breathing room to not let anxiety even surface because we are already engaged in higher vibrational activity, you are above it.

PHASE FOUR

A New Sense of Self

Support Systems

The Universal Support System

One of the greatest shifts than can occur to anyone is the internalization of the concept of oneness. We all can grasp it intellectually on some level, but when you truly feel it from the inside you have accomplished a tremendous shift, and anxiety is going to play a much smaller part in your life.

If you believe in nothing, that nothing exists beyond what is seen with your own eyes, then you need to go further along the path of life with open eyes because if you believe in nothing, you have shut your eyes to the world around you. If you truly are an explorer of knowledge and science, and learn more and more about physics, biology, chemistry, are you truly seeing it with open eyes and seeing the wonder and intelligence in it? There is consciousness behind everything. Start approaching life in this way and let go of traditional views vs. yours; simply develop your own observation of life and be really open beyond the dogma you have been preached, whether to believe or not to believe in something. Develop your own critical, yet open view on everything. Remember that just because it is unseen to science right now, does not mean it does not exist.

If you truly take the scientific method, hypothesis, measurable results, and repetition, you will know that when I tell you that I have seen and measured as a practitioner, through hundreds of people, including myself, and complete strangers, witnessed other practitioners do similar things to other people I don't know, that is, in sum, a version of the scientific method. That means that a certain part of our human experience is measurable and repeatable with people that believe it or not. That means there is something in it. Whether you can touch it or measure it with a tool, or measure it based on self-observation like most of psychological assessments, you can feel happy, sad, in love. Can you measure how much a person is in love? Can you prove in a lab if someone experiences love? No, but it is such a common and significant part of our human experience that we simply agree to its existence. So why do some people put their blinders on and refuse to believe in something that is as immeasurable in a lab as the concept of love. You can measure the physical reaction to love, but you cannot really measure love. In the same way when you hear of concepts such as spirit guides, why be so stiff and refuse the concept just because we do not possess any instrumentation of measuring it?

I was like that. I grew up in an atheistic house, didn't believe in anything and was proud of it, too. I had great philosophical debates supporting this point of view, rejecting all religions. Yet, in my early twenties I started shifting this stubborn approach and decided to take a critical, yet open approach to life and beyond. I didn't start believing in everything, but started opening myself up to the possibility, and making a sound decision with time on each matter at hand. I still enjoy my belief in the soul, and source consciousness, free of religious structure and made it my own. I encourage you to do your own self-examination free of outside influences. This will strengthen you in whatever path you choose to take. Blind belief is a problem, no belief, is still a belief, just a belief in nothing, and it is still blind.

Please allow this statement to open your mind, not as a source of comfort but as welcoming truth that you may acknowledge now, or sometime in the future, it is your choice: you have the free will. Once you realize this and truly internalize it, then you will be able to realize your true potential and enjoy a more flowing version of your life. This is not comfort for the feeble mind, this is the realization of how this universe works, and you can start using it for the advancement of your highest good, which at its purest will always be for the highest good of the entire world. Take a moment and be open to this possibility, it is your free will to accept it or not.

The universe is you, not apart from you. Source is you, and you are part of the source consciousness. You are a co-creator of your so called life.

You are an integral part of this universe, not separate from it. This is one of the hardest concepts to teach people of Judeo-Christian backgrounds, because they believe in separation from the God or the universe. They believe God is a separate entity that is either judging them, assessing, or worse, punishing them in some way. Treating them like rascally children.

Grasp the idea that the universe, that Omni-consciousness, or all that is, is really all that is. The belief that God or the source creator separated parts of itself to create us is erroneous. I know that this would usually require a longer conversation on this subject, however it is time to accept that God, Creator, universe, source whatever you choose to believe in, exists within us. It is us. We are like leaves on a never-ending tree. We feel so far from our source not realizing that we are part of it. Realizing that the leaf from the next branch seems so far away and distant, yet it is just another being very similar to me. There is no separation, you are an expression of source.

If you would truly absorb the scientific approach of quantum physics that everything is energy, you will have an easier time getting that we are not separated from our environment in any way. What we are, is a conscious collection of energy that takes form in this dimension as a human body, mind and spirit, but is not limited to this manifestation in any way. The visual I like to bring within your mind now is that moment in the movie "The Matrix" in which Neo saw how things truly are. In this case, he saw them as ones, and zeros. At this point he became the master of this so-called reality. Similarly, and probably without the martial arts portion, you can become the master of your reality once you understand you have the power not only over reality, but creating the reality.

As Carl Jung brought to the west the idea of collective unconsciousness over a hundred year ago, we can start seeing the beauty in it beyond the intellectual idea behind it and start using it for the advancement of our personal life. There is a universal matrix of consciousness that we are part of; we simply need to know that we can tap into this field of consciousness and become a powerful positive creator of thoughts, feelings, concepts, and bend it to serve the highest good.

So how is all this related to you and anxiety?

You are not alone. You are never alone. You are always a part of the greater reality and matrix.

The sense of separation leads to anxiousness. Only when you feel alone and separated can you feel anxious. It is an illusion of separateness. You are part of this greater universe and part of this greater consciousness that we call humanity and this consciousness grows further into higher and higher levels, back to source.

You are not a silent partner in it, either. You have the power to shift and change things with your consciousness, because this consciousness is directly linked to all that is, and we constantly manipulate it with our thoughts, feelings, and desires. Please don't get stuck on desiring to be part of the one, because it is as silly as sitting on your couch, really wishing to be human, you already are.

When you ask for protection and help you will receive it!

When you are doing things that serve your own highest good, following your inner compass that is not influenced by fear, doubt, and social expectations, you will experience a relief from anxiety in the long run. Because you are ultimately doing what you were supposed to when you planned this life before you came down into it and placed the veil of ignorance on your awareness.

Please know, you are one with everything that is, and the more you do meditation and exercises that expand on this you will feel more and more at ease with your role and the life that you chose to have on this planet. Anxiety will simply dissolve away.

I want to repeat that this shift in consciousness is not merely to calm and comfort you. The reason it calms you is because it is your truth. That inner knowing that you are close to your true self, calms you. This is not falsehood, this is truth. When you feel truth in my words you will feel the reverberation of it going through your body, mind, heart, and soul. It just feels good.

The world and the universe are not working against you in any way shape or form. It is you that is working against the natural flow of your own life. Resistance, instilled by fear, and your desire to control life in a forced manner, not out of personal power, but out of fear. Everything feels more difficult that way, there is greater resistance to everything you do, and you can feel it. If you feel resistance, it is because you have created it. I am not saying life should be without challenge, but the resistance in it is self-made and completely unnecessary.

I like to put it this way. If you feel resistance, it is your heart and subconscious mind, reminding you that you are on the wrong path or simply doing things in the wrong way. Release the fear and judgment, and you will start flowing in the right direction. As Abraham says through Esther Hicks, "If you are struggling to go up stream in the river of life, it is because you are going the wrong way. Simply turn the boat and go with the flow, it is effortless."

The Human Support system

The sense of safety we receive from the universe and fellow humans is vital to dissolving anxiety. The lack of it will instill fear and anxiety in the deepest, most elemental core of our being. This is one of the most important and comprehensive shifts that needs to take place in your perception of the world.

We also need to know that there is someone out there that will be there for us. We are social creatures. We do not do well without social interaction, support, or perspective. Some people enjoy solitude and do well with it, however, most people need more.

The most important aspect of a support network is that you FEEL that you have support. People become more and more confident in life when then know that they are not alone. Safety in the world is a basic confidence builder. That is how we develop healthy children, they can move away from us at a playground when they feel safe and know you will be there for them. If they lose you out of sight, they know you are there. If you move away from that spot and they can't see you, they will panic and feel incapable of relaxing and playing. The emergency of finding their support and source of safety in the world supersedes their urge to play, and they will experience the anxiety of abandonment, no matter how short.

As adults, we know that we are okay in the world, but do we really feel that we have that support, that at the end of the day you can talk to someone, either in person or over the phone who will listen to you, make you feel understood, that will support you unconditionally. If you don't have someone like that in your personal circle, don't worry you can always find professional help. This is an important role that counselors and therapists fill for many.

There is no limit on who it can be, partner, friend, neighbor, cousin, mother, father, siblings, daughter, son, therapist. If you are feeling the need to be understood, supported, create this support system for yourself; don't just sit idly and feel anxious and alone.

Integration of a New Self

Ultimately when you master this concept of support and safety, you become truly one with yourself and the universe. You will know that you do not need anyone else's support because you will feel fully supported by the universe, your guides, and your soul. You still enjoy the company of others, sharing your dreams and experiences, but you don't do it out of necessity but out of love and joy.

The sense of safety comes from the deep knowing that you are here with a purpose, you are doing it with joy and passion, and knowing that you have the time to do it. When time runs out for you, you will exit in a manner that you choose (one of your pre-planned exit point to this life), all fear is gone from your system. You are experiencing full Self Mastery. Your mission transcends now to being an inspiration and teacher to others.

You are FREE. The world is your oyster.

Until you reach that point, you may rely on the support of others, don't be too proud; it will only hold you back. It is silly not to receive assistance when needed whether you are aware of it or not.

Self-Mastery is rarely achieved by yourself without the assistance, support, and inspirations of others.

I work with people an entire year and most reach this level or close to it in that period of time, if they truly intend to change. It is possible and doable to shift this dramatically in a year. You do need to work on yourself, but it does not mean it is hard. Life flows in easier ways. Things just come to be. Synchronicity fills your daily life, you live with joy and the pure wonder at how beautiful life is. You notice the beauty in everything and everyone. You become less judgmental of others and self. It simply comes to be. This is part of everyone's journey and can be reached and maintained.

Don't think that living life this way is unattainable. Remember earlier I wrote that Deepak Chopra's book *The Seven Spiritual Laws of Success* first seemed out of reach, then through internal work and shifting I got closer and closer. You don't suddenly appear there or not, it is something that can be reached in a progressive manner, filled with dozens of a-ha moments and fluctuations that eventually trend upwards into a better and better version of yourself. You don't stop being you, quite the opposite, just a cleaner freer version of yourself. Without the garbage, baggage, and limiting beliefs. Recognizing your greater self in a process of expansion and growth.

You become YOU!

Conclusion

It is within your power to shift and change for the better. Anxiety is a mal-adaption that can be corrected. It is a mishandling and misunderstanding of your own greatness. You can regain your mastery over life and tread this earth with calm and confidence, in yourself, and the world.

This book is just the beginning of this journey into mastery and freedom from anxiety. Embark in this journey for it is your journey and no one else's. No one can do this for you but you. The universe places the right book, the right person and the right coincidence for you to realize and grow. Embrace the possibilities that lie within you, even if you cannot see it from this vantage point of here and now. It is yours, it is you, seeking a way to authenticity, growth, and expansion of your being.

About the author

Harry Kroner is the founder and director of *New Awareness Institute*. He is the creator of cutting edge programs such as; *Freedom from Anxiety, Deep Personal Healing, and Soul Healing.* He brings a unique blend of healing to all levels of your being; body, heart, mind, and soul. He has become a leading expert in soul healing, and deep emotional healing.

He is a graduate of the University of Massachusetts in Psychology, and received extensive training in hypnotherapy, energy psychology, life coaching, NLP, energy healing, Quantum Healing Hypnosis Technique, and more.

Harry has helped thousands of individuals reach happier, more balanced, and wiser versions of themselves. Helping many bring peace into their lives in his office in Prescott Arizona. As well, as around the country and the world, through phone and Skype sessions. In addition to working with individuals, he conducts workshops, seminars, and retreats to groups bringing his teachings, healing processes, personal growth, and insight to many more.

For more information please contact him directly at:
harry@NewAwarenessInstitute.com
(928) 248-8372

Printed in the United States
By Bookmasters